AI and the Circular Economy: Transforming Sustainability with Intelligent Systems

Copyright

AI and the Circular Economy: Transforming Sustainability with Intelligent Systems

Published by Global Climate Solutions

ISBN: 978-1-991369-09-3 (eBook)

ISBN: 978-1-991369-10-9 (Paperback)

Table of Contents

Preface

The transition from a linear economy to a circular economy represents one of the most significant shifts in global economic and environmental policy. With rising pressure to reduce waste, conserve resources, and mitigate climate change, industries worldwide are seeking innovative solutions to achieve sustainability without compromising efficiency or profitability. At the heart of this transformation lies artificial intelligence (AI)—a powerful tool that is revolutionizing how we manage materials, optimize production, and design for longevity.

AI and the Circular Economy: Transforming Sustainability with Intelligent Systems explores the intersection of technology, sustainability, and business strategy, demonstrating how AI is reshaping industries by enabling real-time data analysis, predictive modeling, smart automation, and blockchain-based transparency. The ability to anticipate material flows, reduce inefficiencies, and enhance decision-making is no longer a futuristic vision—it is happening now, with AI at the forefront of sustainable innovation.

This book presents a forward-looking perspective on how AI-driven tools can accelerate circular economy practices across sectors, from manufacturing and retail to construction and waste management. It provides critical insights into the challenges and opportunities presented by AI adoption, offering a roadmap for businesses, policymakers, and sustainability professionals to harness these technologies effectively.

The future of sustainability will be defined by how well we integrate intelligence into our resource management systems. By embracing AI-driven circularity, we can create resilient economies, minimize environmental impact, and unlock new pathways for sustainable growth. The question is no longer if AI will shape the circular economy, but how quickly we can leverage its full potential.

Robert C. Brears

Introduction

The global economy is at a crossroads. Decades of reliance on a linear model—take, make, dispose—have led to alarming levels of resource depletion and waste generation. As the environmental and economic consequences of this unsustainable approach become increasingly apparent, the transition to a circular economy (CE) has emerged as a critical solution. Unlike the traditional linear system, the CE seeks to create a closed-loop system where waste is minimized, resources are reused, and materials retain their value for as long as possible.

Artificial intelligence (AI) is poised to play a transformative role in this shift. By providing powerful tools for optimizing resource use, enhancing efficiency, and minimizing waste, AI offers unprecedented opportunities to advance CE principles. However, integrating AI into these systems presents unique challenges, from ethical considerations to technological gaps.

This book explores how AI can be leveraged to optimize resource use and minimize waste within a CE framework. It provides a comprehensive analysis of AI's applications, challenges, and potential across various sectors, offering a vision for a more sustainable future. The journey begins by laying the groundwork for understanding the synergy between AI and the CE, setting the stage for an in-depth exploration of key themes and strategies.

Overview of the Circular Economy

The CE represents a transformative approach to global economic systems, fundamentally reshaping how resources are used and valued. Unlike the traditional linear model of production and consumption, which follows the path of "take, make, dispose," CE emphasizes closing the loop on material and resource flows. This is achieved through strategies such as reuse, recycling, remanufacturing, and the extension of product life cycles. The primary goal is to minimize waste and create sustainable systems where resources are continuously cycled back into productive use.

At its core, CE challenges the paradigm of resource scarcity and waste management. It shifts focus toward designing out waste from the beginning of the production process, ensuring that products are not only durable and repairable but also capable of being easily disassembled for material recovery. This concept addresses critical global challenges, including environmental degradation, resource depletion, and the growing impact of climate change. As industries and governments adopt CE principles, they are moving toward economic systems that balance environmental, social, and economic priorities.

The adoption of CE is driven by several factors, including increasing resource scarcity, regulatory pressure, and rising consumer demand for sustainable products. Businesses are recognizing the competitive advantages of transitioning to circular models, such as reducing costs, enhancing brand value, and fostering innovation. Governments are implementing policies to encourage CE practices, from tax incentives for recycling to bans on single-use plastics. The result is a growing alignment of interests among stakeholders, creating momentum for systemic change.

CE operates across multiple levels, from individual products to entire systems. On the micro level, businesses redesign products to be modular, repairable, and recyclable. At the meso level, industries form eco-industrial parks where waste from one company becomes input for another. On the macro level, governments and cities implement policies and infrastructures that support resource recovery and sustainable practices. This multi-level approach highlights the interconnectedness of efforts required to realize the full potential of CE.

However, transitioning to CE is not without challenges. One of the most significant barriers is the need for a mindset shift among consumers, businesses, and policymakers. Additionally, existing infrastructures are often designed for linear systems, requiring substantial investment and innovation to adapt. Despite these obstacles, the urgency of addressing global resource and environmental challenges underscores the need for accelerated adoption of CE principles.

In the context of CE, digital technologies such as AI play a pivotal role in optimizing resource use and minimizing waste. By enabling precision in resource management, enhancing product design, and driving innovation in waste recovery, AI accelerates the implementation of CE principles. As the book progresses, the transformative potential of AI in CE will become a recurring theme, showcasing its ability to drive systemic change in how we produce, consume, and manage resources.

In summary, the CE is a powerful framework for addressing the world's most pressing environmental and resource challenges. Its principles offer a pathway to sustainable economic systems that prioritize resilience, efficiency, and equity. As the integration of AI into CE practices unfolds, it presents new opportunities to enhance these outcomes and overcome traditional barriers to circularity.

Role of AI in Advancing Circular Economy Principles

AI has emerged as a transformative force in reshaping industries and economies worldwide. Within the framework of the CE, AI offers powerful tools to optimize resource use, improve efficiency, and eliminate waste, accelerating the transition from linear to circular systems. By enabling advanced data analytics, machine learning (ML), and predictive modeling, AI enhances the capacity of businesses and policymakers to implement CE principles effectively.

One of the core contributions of AI to CE is its ability to provide deep insights into resource flows. AI-driven data analytics can map, monitor, and predict the movement of materials and products across supply chains. By identifying inefficiencies, redundancies, and opportunities for material reuse, AI helps organizations make informed decisions that align with CE goals. This ability to track resources in real time ensures that materials remain in circulation for as long as possible, reducing waste and conserving natural resources.

AI also plays a pivotal role in optimizing product design for circularity. Through generative design tools, AI enables designers and engineers to create products that are modular, durable, and easily disassembled. These tools use algorithms to analyze design options and recommend configurations that minimize material use while maximizing product lifespan. This ensures that products are not only more sustainable but also easier to repair, upgrade, and recycle, directly supporting CE objectives.

In manufacturing, AI contributes to waste reduction and resource efficiency. Advanced ML algorithms optimize production processes by identifying patterns and anomalies that lead to material loss or energy inefficiency. AI-powered systems can also predict equipment maintenance needs, preventing unexpected breakdowns and minimizing downtime. This predictive maintenance capability extends the life of machinery, reduces resource consumption, and aligns manufacturing processes with CE principles.

AI's impact extends beyond production to consumption and end-of-life management. In consumer-facing industries, AI-driven platforms enable personalized recommendations for sustainable consumption, encouraging consumers to choose products and services that align with CE values. At the same time, AI supports the development of sharing and leasing models by managing the logistics of shared assets and ensuring optimal utilization.

In the waste management sector, AI technologies such as computer vision and ML are revolutionizing recycling and resource recovery. AI-powered systems can accurately identify, sort, and separate materials in waste streams, improving recycling efficiency and reducing contamination. These systems enhance the scalability of waste recovery efforts, making it possible to process larger volumes of material with greater precision and speed.

AI also facilitates circular supply chain management by providing end-to-end visibility and optimization. By integrating data from multiple sources, AI enables businesses to track products and materials throughout their lifecycle, ensuring adherence to CE principles. AI-driven platforms can predict demand, optimize inventory, and manage reverse logistics, ensuring that materials flow seamlessly through the supply chain and back into production cycles.

In addition to operational benefits, AI supports strategic decision-making for CE adoption. Predictive analytics and scenario modeling allow businesses and governments to evaluate the potential outcomes of CE initiatives, helping them prioritize actions and allocate resources effectively. By reducing uncertainty and enhancing decision-making, AI strengthens the foundation for a successful transition to circular systems.

Through these capabilities, AI not only advances CE principles but also unlocks new opportunities for innovation and collaboration, making it a cornerstone of the transition to sustainable economic systems.

Key Challenges in Resource Optimization and Waste Minimization

Resource optimization and waste minimization are fundamental pillars of the CE. However, the transition from a linear economy to a circular system presents significant challenges. These obstacles stem from technical, economic, social, and regulatory factors that hinder the effective implementation of CE principles.

One of the foremost challenges in resource optimization is the complexity of supply chains. In many industries, supply chains are global and involve multiple stakeholders. This complexity makes it difficult to map resource flows accurately, identify inefficiencies, and pinpoint opportunities for optimization. A lack of transparency and real-time data across supply chains exacerbates these issues, creating barriers to achieving circularity.

Another challenge is the design and production of products that align with CE principles. Most products today are not designed with reuse, repair, or recycling in mind. Instead, they are optimized for short-term functionality and cost efficiency. Transitioning to a design philosophy that prioritizes circularity requires significant investment in research and development, as well as a cultural shift within organizations. Additionally, industries often face resistance to change due to entrenched practices and a lack of awareness about the benefits of circular product design.

The economic feasibility of resource optimization and waste minimization is another critical hurdle. Adopting CE practices often involves upfront costs, such as investing in new technologies, redesigning products, or overhauling production processes. For many businesses, especially small and medium-sized enterprises (SMEs), these costs can be prohibitive. Furthermore, the financial benefits of CE practices, such as cost savings from resource efficiency, are often realized only in the long term, creating a disincentive for immediate action.

Consumer behavior also poses a significant challenge. Achieving resource optimization and waste minimization requires active participation from consumers, who play a crucial role in choosing sustainable products, adopting sharing or leasing models, and correctly disposing of materials. However, a lack of awareness and education about the importance of circularity often leads to resistance or indifference. In addition, convenience and affordability often take precedence over sustainability in consumer decision-making, further complicating efforts to drive change.

Regulatory and policy frameworks are another area of concern. In many regions, existing regulations are designed to support linear economic models, creating obstacles to the adoption of CE principles. For example, waste disposal may be cheaper and easier than implementing recycling programs due to inadequate regulatory incentives. Moreover, inconsistent policies across jurisdictions create challenges for businesses operating in multiple markets, as they must navigate a patchwork of regulations.

Technological limitations also hinder resource optimization and waste minimization. While technologies such as AI and advanced recycling systems offer significant potential, their adoption is often constrained by high costs, lack of technical expertise, and insufficient infrastructure. In particular, developing countries face additional barriers, such as limited access to technology and funding, which further widen the gap in CE implementation.

Finally, the lack of standardized metrics and benchmarks for measuring resource optimization and waste minimization complicates efforts to track progress and assess the effectiveness of CE initiatives. Without clear and universally accepted metrics, it is challenging for businesses and policymakers to set goals, monitor outcomes, and identify areas for improvement.

Addressing these challenges requires a coordinated effort among governments, businesses, and consumers. Overcoming technical, economic, and regulatory barriers will be essential to unlocking the full potential of resource optimization and waste minimization in the CE.

Objective and Structure of the Book

The primary objective of this book is to explore the transformative potential of AI in advancing the principles of the CE. With the global economy facing unprecedented challenges related to resource depletion, environmental degradation, and waste accumulation, the integration of AI into CE frameworks offers a pathway to more sustainable and efficient systems. This book aims to provide a comprehensive understanding of how AI can optimize resource use, minimize waste, and support the transition to circular systems.

By leveraging AI, industries and governments can overcome many of the barriers associated with implementing CE principles. The book delves into the ways AI enhances transparency, efficiency, and decision-making in resource management and waste reduction. It seeks to bridge the gap between theoretical discussions of CE and practical applications, offering insights into how AI tools and technologies can facilitate this transition. Through an analysis of AI-driven approaches, the book sheds light on the potential for AI to not only accelerate CE adoption but also address the systemic challenges that hinder progress.

The structure of the book is designed to guide readers through the multifaceted relationship between AI and CE, presenting a logical progression of concepts, strategies, and solutions. The introductory section provides an overview of the CE framework, the role of AI, and the challenges in resource optimization and waste minimization. These foundational chapters establish the context and set the stage for a deeper exploration of AI's contributions.

The first chapter, "Foundations of the Circular Economy and AI," introduces the principles of CE and outlines the fundamental concepts of AI. It discusses the intersection of these two domains, highlighting the synergies and opportunities they create. This chapter serves as a primer for readers unfamiliar with the technical and conceptual aspects of CE and AI.

Subsequent chapters are organized around specific applications of AI within CE. Chapter two, "AI in Resource Optimization," focuses on how AI tools enable efficient resource mapping, demand forecasting, and material flow optimization. It provides a detailed analysis of AI-driven strategies for enhancing resource efficiency. Chapter three, "AI for Waste Minimization," examines AI applications in waste identification, recycling, and recovery processes, demonstrating how AI can reduce material losses across industries.

Chapter four, "AI in Sustainable Product Design," addresses how AI-driven tools support the development of modular, durable, and recyclable products. This chapter emphasizes the importance of integrating CE principles into the design phase. Chapter five, "AI-Driven Business Models in the Circular Economy," explores innovative AI-enabled business models such as sharing platforms and subscription-based systems, highlighting their role in advancing circular practices.

Chapter six, "AI and Circular Supply Chains," investigates how AI enhances supply chain transparency and supports circular procurement processes. The seventh chapter, "Ethical and Governance Considerations," delves into the ethical implications and regulatory challenges of using AI in CE systems. Finally, chapter eight, "Future Directions and Innovations," outlines emerging AI technologies and their potential to drive further advancements in CE.

The conclusion ties together the insights presented throughout the book, reinforcing the importance of AI in achieving a sustainable, circular future. By examining the opportunities and challenges at the intersection of AI and CE, this book provides a roadmap for leveraging technology to create a more resilient and sustainable global economy.

Chapter 1: Foundations of the Circular Economy and AI

The CE represents a significant shift in how resources are used, emphasizing the creation of closed-loop systems where waste is minimized, and materials are reused. At the same time, AI has emerged as a transformative technology, capable of enhancing decision-making, optimizing processes, and driving innovation. This chapter lays the groundwork for understanding the fundamental principles of CE and AI, examining their intersections and potential synergies. By exploring the core concepts of both fields, this chapter sets the stage for a deeper dive into how AI can advance CE objectives in practical and impactful ways.

Defining the Circular Economy: Principles and Benefits

The CE is an economic model designed to address the environmental and resource-related challenges posed by the traditional linear economy, which follows the "take, make, dispose" paradigm. CE emphasizes the importance of maintaining the value of products, materials, and resources for as long as possible while minimizing waste and environmental impact. By fundamentally rethinking how resources are utilized and reused, CE provides a framework for creating sustainable systems that balance economic growth with environmental stewardship.

At its core, the CE operates on three primary principles: designing out waste and pollution, keeping products and materials in use, and regenerating natural systems. These principles provide a foundation for transforming industries and economies, creating a shift toward resource efficiency and sustainability.

Designing Out Waste and Pollution

One of the key principles of CE is to design waste and pollution out of systems from the outset. In a linear economy, waste is often an inevitable byproduct of production and consumption, with significant environmental and economic costs. CE challenges this notion by advocating for systems and processes that eliminate waste at every stage of a product's lifecycle.

This involves rethinking product design to ensure that materials are used efficiently and can be recovered or reused after the product's initial use. For example, modular design allows products to be easily repaired or upgraded, extending their lifespan and reducing the need for new resources. Similarly, adopting non-toxic and biodegradable materials ensures that any waste generated can be safely reintegrated into natural systems, reducing pollution and environmental harm.

Keeping Products and Materials in Use

A central tenet of CE is the concept of maintaining the value of products and materials for as long as possible. This is achieved through strategies such as reuse, repair, remanufacturing, and recycling. By keeping materials in circulation, CE reduces the demand for virgin resources and minimizes waste generation.

For businesses, this principle presents opportunities to create new revenue streams and reduce costs. For example, companies can offer repair or refurbishment services, enabling consumers to extend the life of their products rather than replacing them. Similarly, recycling allows materials to be recovered and reintroduced into production cycles, reducing reliance on raw material extraction.

The sharing economy is another example of how CE keeps products in use. Platforms that enable sharing, renting, or leasing products maximize the utilization of resources and reduce the need for new production. These models align with CE principles by shifting the focus from ownership to access, encouraging more efficient use of resources.

Regenerating Natural Systems

Unlike the linear economy, which depletes resources and degrades ecosystems, CE aims to regenerate natural systems. This involves restoring and enhancing ecosystems to ensure the long-term availability of resources. Practices such as regenerative agriculture, reforestation, and habitat restoration contribute to the replenishment of natural systems and improve biodiversity.

In addition to environmental benefits, regenerating natural systems has significant economic and social advantages. Healthy ecosystems provide essential services, such as clean air and water, fertile soil, and climate regulation, which are vital for human well-being and economic stability. By integrating these practices into economic systems, CE promotes a sustainable balance between human activity and the environment.

Economic and Environmental Benefits of the Circular Economy

The adoption of CE principles offers a wide range of benefits for businesses, governments, and society as a whole. From an economic perspective, CE reduces costs by improving resource efficiency and minimizing waste. Businesses that embrace CE principles can gain a competitive advantage by reducing material costs, enhancing brand value, and driving innovation in product and service offerings.

CE also creates opportunities for job creation and economic diversification. Sectors such as recycling, repair, and remanufacturing generate employment while fostering skills development and local economic growth. Additionally, CE encourages innovation by driving the development of new technologies, processes, and business models that support resource efficiency and sustainability.

From an environmental standpoint, CE mitigates many of the negative impacts associated with the linear economy. By reducing resource extraction and waste generation, CE decreases greenhouse gas emissions and minimizes pollution. It also helps to address global challenges such as resource scarcity and climate change, contributing to a more resilient and sustainable future.

Social Benefits and Broader Impacts

CE's benefits extend beyond economic and environmental outcomes to include significant social advantages. By promoting sustainable consumption and production patterns, CE enhances quality of life and reduces inequalities. For example, sharing economy models provide access to goods and services for individuals who might not otherwise afford them, fostering inclusivity and equity.

Moreover, CE contributes to the health and well-being of communities by reducing pollution and environmental degradation. Cleaner air, water, and ecosystems translate into better public health outcomes and improved living conditions, particularly for vulnerable populations disproportionately affected by environmental harm.

Introduction to Artificial Intelligence: Key Concepts and Applications

AI is a transformative technology that mimics human intelligence to perform tasks such as learning, reasoning, problem-solving, and decision-making. Rooted in computer science, AI leverages algorithms, data processing, and computational power to analyze information, detect patterns, and provide actionable insights. While AI has been in development for decades, recent advancements in ML, neural networks, and data availability have significantly expanded its capabilities and applications across industries.

AI can be broadly classified into three categories: narrow AI, general AI, and superintelligent AI. Narrow AI, also known as weak AI, is designed to perform specific tasks and is the most prevalent form of AI today. Examples include virtual assistants, facial recognition systems, and recommendation algorithms. General AI, or strong AI, represents systems with the ability to perform any intellectual task that a human can do. Although it remains theoretical, it is a key area of research. Superintelligent AI, which surpasses human intelligence in all aspects, is a concept explored primarily in academic and ethical discussions.

Key Components of AI

AI systems are built on several foundational components that enable them to process data and perform tasks effectively:

- **Machine Learning:** ML is a subset of AI that enables systems to learn and improve from experience without explicit programming. ML algorithms analyze large datasets to identify patterns and make predictions or decisions. Applications include fraud detection, customer behavior analysis, and predictive maintenance.
- **Natural Language Processing (NLP):** NLP allows AI systems to understand, interpret, and respond to human language. By analyzing text or speech, NLP enables applications such as chatbots, language translation, and sentiment analysis. This component is critical for improving human-computer interaction.
- **Computer Vision:** Computer vision enables AI to process and analyze visual data, such as images and videos. It is widely used in facial recognition, autonomous vehicles, and quality control in manufacturing.
- **Neural Networks:** Neural networks are algorithms modeled after the human brain's structure. They are the backbone of deep learning, a subset of AI that excels in tasks requiring complex data analysis, such as image recognition and language processing.
- **Robotics:** Robotics integrates AI into physical machines to perform tasks that require precision and automation. Applications range from industrial robots in manufacturing to autonomous drones and robotic surgery.

Applications of AI Across Industries

AI's versatility has led to its adoption across a wide range of industries, revolutionizing processes and enabling new opportunities:

- **Healthcare:** AI enhances diagnostic accuracy, personalizes treatment plans, and streamlines administrative processes. Applications include medical imaging, drug discovery, and virtual health assistants.
- **Finance:** Financial institutions use AI for fraud detection, credit scoring, algorithmic trading, and customer service. By automating data analysis, AI improves decision-making and operational efficiency.
- **Manufacturing:** AI optimizes production processes through predictive maintenance, quality control, and supply chain management. Smart factories leverage AI to enhance efficiency and reduce waste.
- **Retail:** AI powers personalized recommendations, dynamic pricing, and inventory optimization in the retail sector. Chatbots and virtual assistants enhance customer experiences by providing real-time support.
- **Transportation:** AI supports autonomous vehicles, traffic management, and route optimization. These applications improve safety, efficiency, and sustainability in transportation systems.
- **Energy:** In the energy sector, AI is used for demand forecasting, grid optimization, and renewable energy integration. It enables more efficient resource use and supports the transition to sustainable energy systems.

Challenges and Ethical Considerations

Despite its potential, AI presents challenges and ethical concerns that require careful consideration. Issues such as data privacy, algorithmic bias, and job displacement highlight the need for responsible development and deployment of AI systems. Ensuring transparency, fairness, and accountability in AI applications is critical to maximizing its benefits while mitigating risks.

AI's transformative potential is undeniable, with its ability to process complex data and enhance decision-making across industries. As this book explores the role of AI in advancing the CE, these foundational concepts will serve as a basis for understanding its applications and impact in optimizing resource use and minimizing waste.

Intersection of AI and the Circular Economy: Opportunities and Synergies

The intersection of AI and the CE offers transformative opportunities to address the pressing challenges of resource depletion, waste generation, and environmental degradation. By leveraging AI's ability to process vast amounts of data, optimize processes, and provide actionable insights, businesses and policymakers can implement CE principles with greater efficiency and precision. This convergence of AI and CE creates synergies that enhance resource use, minimize waste, and foster innovation across industries.

Optimizing Resource Efficiency

AI is uniquely positioned to improve resource efficiency, a core tenet of the CE. Through advanced analytics and ML algorithms, AI enables the mapping and monitoring of resource flows across complex supply chains. By identifying inefficiencies, redundancies, and opportunities for material reuse, AI enhances decision-making in resource management.

For instance, predictive analytics powered by AI can forecast demand for materials and products, reducing overproduction and minimizing waste. Similarly, AI-enabled systems can optimize production processes to use resources more effectively, ensuring that inputs are utilized to their fullest potential. These capabilities align directly with CE goals, supporting the shift from linear to circular systems.

Enhancing Product Lifecycle Management

AI plays a critical role in managing the lifecycle of products, from design to end-of-life. Generative design tools powered by AI allow engineers to create products that are modular, durable, and easily recyclable. These tools analyze various design parameters and recommend configurations that minimize material use and maximize product longevity, reducing the need for resource-intensive manufacturing.

AI also supports predictive maintenance, which extends the lifespan of products and equipment. By analyzing real-time data from sensors and systems, AI identifies potential issues before they lead to failures, preventing unnecessary replacements and reducing waste. This proactive approach ensures that products remain functional for longer, contributing to the circular flow of materials.

At the end-of-life stage, AI enhances recycling and resource recovery processes. Computer vision and ML algorithms can accurately identify and sort materials, improving the efficiency and effectiveness of recycling systems. This not only reduces the volume of waste sent to landfills but also ensures that valuable resources are recovered and reintroduced into production cycles.

Supporting Circular Business Models

The integration of AI into circular business models creates new opportunities for innovation and value creation. AI-driven platforms enable sharing and leasing models by managing the logistics of shared assets, ensuring optimal utilization and minimizing resource consumption. These platforms use data to match supply with demand, streamline operations, and provide personalized experiences for users.

In subscription-based models, AI enhances customer engagement by analyzing preferences and usage patterns to offer tailored services. This fosters long-term relationships between businesses and consumers while promoting sustainable consumption. Reverse logistics, a critical component of CE, also benefits from AI's ability to optimize the collection, sorting, and redistribution of used products and materials.

Improving Waste Management and Recycling

AI revolutionizes waste management by providing advanced tools for waste identification, sorting, and processing. Computer vision systems powered by AI can detect and classify materials in waste streams with high accuracy, enabling efficient sorting and reducing contamination in recycling processes. This ensures that more materials are recovered and reintroduced into production cycles, supporting CE objectives.

ML algorithms also optimize waste collection and transportation, reducing costs and environmental impacts. By analyzing data on waste generation and disposal patterns, AI systems can design efficient collection routes and schedules, minimizing fuel consumption and emissions. These applications demonstrate how AI enhances the scalability and effectiveness of waste management systems, making them more aligned with CE principles.

Enabling Circular Supply Chains

AI fosters circular supply chains by providing end-to-end visibility and optimization. By integrating data from multiple sources, AI systems track products and materials throughout their lifecycle, ensuring transparency and accountability. This enables businesses to identify bottlenecks, reduce inefficiencies, and implement circular procurement practices.

AI also supports the creation of closed-loop supply chains by facilitating the reintegration of recovered materials into production cycles. Predictive analytics and demand forecasting help align supply with demand, ensuring that resources are used efficiently and sustainably. These capabilities strengthen the resilience of supply chains and reduce reliance on virgin materials.

Driving Innovation and Collaboration

The convergence of AI and CE unlocks new opportunities for innovation and collaboration. AI's ability to analyze complex datasets and identify patterns supports the development of novel solutions to resource and waste challenges. For example, AI can identify previously untapped opportunities for material reuse or recovery, driving advancements in sustainable technologies.

Collaboration among stakeholders is essential for implementing CE principles at scale, and AI facilitates this by providing shared platforms for data exchange and coordination. Businesses, governments, and researchers can use AI-driven tools to align their efforts, share best practices, and develop integrated strategies for circularity.

Addressing Challenges and Ethical Considerations

While the integration of AI and CE presents significant opportunities, it also raises challenges that must be addressed. Issues such as data privacy, algorithmic bias, and technological access highlight the need for ethical and inclusive approaches to AI development and deployment. Ensuring that AI applications align with CE values requires careful consideration of these factors.

The intersection of AI and CE represents a powerful synergy with the potential to transform how resources are used and valued. By leveraging AI's capabilities to optimize processes, enhance efficiency, and foster innovation, stakeholders can accelerate the transition to a CE, paving the way for a more sustainable and resilient future.

Challenges in Integrating AI with Circular Economy Strategies

While AI has the potential to significantly advance CE strategies, its integration is not without challenges. These obstacles stem from technological, economic, social, and regulatory dimensions, requiring careful consideration and resolution to fully leverage AI's potential in achieving circularity.

Data Availability and Quality

One of the primary challenges in integrating AI with CE strategies is the availability and quality of data. AI relies on large datasets to train algorithms and generate insights. However, many industries lack access to comprehensive, accurate, and standardized data on resource flows, material properties, and waste generation. This data scarcity limits AI's effectiveness in optimizing CE practices.

Even when data is available, it may be fragmented across supply chains, making it difficult to consolidate and analyze. The lack of standardized data formats and interoperability between systems further exacerbates the issue, hindering the ability of AI to provide actionable insights. Ensuring data quality and consistency is a critical prerequisite for successful AI integration in CE initiatives.

High Implementation Costs

Implementing AI solutions in CE systems often involves significant upfront investment in technology, infrastructure, and expertise. SMEs, which are key players in many industries, may find these costs prohibitive. AI systems require advanced hardware, software, and skilled personnel to design, deploy, and maintain, which can strain the resources of smaller organizations.

Moreover, the return on investment (ROI) for AI-driven CE initiatives may take time to materialize, creating a disincentive for businesses to adopt these technologies. Companies may prioritize short-term cost savings over long-term sustainability, delaying the widespread adoption of AI in CE strategies.

Technological Complexity

The technological complexity of AI presents another significant barrier. Developing, deploying, and maintaining AI systems requires specialized expertise in ML, data science, and software engineering. Many organizations lack the technical knowledge and skills necessary to effectively integrate AI into their CE practices.

Additionally, AI algorithms are often perceived as "black boxes" due to their complexity and lack of transparency. This opacity can make it challenging for businesses and stakeholders to trust AI-driven recommendations or understand how decisions are made. Building trust and ensuring transparency in AI systems are essential for their successful integration into CE strategies.

Regulatory and Ethical Concerns

Regulatory frameworks for AI and CE are still evolving, creating uncertainty for businesses and policymakers. Inconsistent regulations across regions can complicate the implementation of AI-driven CE strategies, particularly for organizations operating in multiple markets. Without clear guidelines, businesses may face legal and compliance risks when deploying AI solutions.

Ethical concerns also pose challenges. Issues such as data privacy, algorithmic bias, and the potential for job displacement require careful consideration. Ensuring that AI applications align with ethical principles and societal values is essential for their acceptance and long-term success in supporting CE goals.

Infrastructure and Scalability

The infrastructure required to support AI-driven CE initiatives is often inadequate, particularly in developing regions. AI systems depend on robust digital networks, sensors, and computing resources, which may not be readily available. This digital divide creates disparities in the ability of different regions to implement AI-driven CE solutions, limiting their global scalability.

Even in regions with advanced infrastructure, scaling AI solutions across industries and supply chains presents logistical and operational challenges. The integration of AI systems with existing processes often requires significant modifications, creating disruptions and additional costs.

Resistance to Change

Cultural and organizational resistance to change is a significant barrier to integrating AI with CE strategies. Many businesses and stakeholders are accustomed to linear economic models and may be hesitant to adopt new technologies and practices. Overcoming this inertia requires education, awareness, and a clear demonstration of the benefits of AI-driven CE initiatives.

The integration of AI with CE strategies offers immense potential but requires overcoming these challenges through collaboration, innovation, and targeted investments. Addressing these barriers is essential to unlocking the full potential of AI in driving circularity and sustainability.

Chapter 2: AI in Resource Optimization

Resource optimization lies at the heart of the CE, focusing on minimizing waste and maximizing the utility of materials throughout their lifecycle. AI plays a transformative role in achieving these objectives by leveraging advanced tools such as ML, predictive analytics, and real-time data processing. This chapter explores how AI enables efficient resource mapping, forecasting, and management, empowering industries to align their operations with CE principles. By examining key applications and strategies, this chapter highlights the potential of AI to revolutionize resource use and drive sustainable practices across sectors.

AI for Efficient Resource Mapping and Tracking

Efficient resource mapping and tracking are essential for implementing CE principles, as they provide a clear understanding of material flows and their lifecycle stages. AI significantly enhances these processes by enabling accurate, real-time data collection, analysis, and visualization. Through advanced algorithms, AI helps businesses identify inefficiencies, optimize resource use, and minimize waste.

The Need for Resource Mapping and Tracking

Resource mapping involves identifying the quantity, quality, and location of materials and resources within a system. Tracking extends this process by monitoring the movement of these materials through production, distribution, use, and disposal stages. Together, mapping and tracking create transparency, which is vital for implementing CE strategies such as recycling, remanufacturing, and material recovery.

Traditional resource mapping methods often rely on manual processes or fragmented data, leading to inaccuracies and inefficiencies. AI overcomes these limitations by automating data collection and providing insights that are both precise and actionable. This capability is critical in complex supply chains where materials move across multiple stakeholders and geographies.

AI-Driven Resource Mapping

AI enables resource mapping by integrating data from diverse sources, such as sensors, satellite imagery, and Internet of Things (IoT) devices. ML algorithms process this data to identify patterns and relationships, creating detailed resource maps that provide a comprehensive view of material flows.

For instance, AI-powered geospatial analysis can identify resource hotspots, such as areas with high concentrations of recyclable materials. These maps help businesses and governments prioritize actions, such as establishing recycling centers or optimizing collection routes. Similarly, AI tools can analyze industrial processes to identify where resources are being wasted or underutilized, enabling targeted interventions to improve efficiency.

AI also facilitates dynamic resource mapping, which updates in real-time as new data becomes available. This is particularly useful in industries with rapidly changing conditions, such as agriculture or manufacturing. Dynamic mapping allows organizations to respond quickly to shifts in resource availability, ensuring that materials are used efficiently and waste is minimized.

AI for Real-Time Tracking

Tracking resources in real time is crucial for maintaining transparency and accountability across supply chains. AI enhances tracking by integrating data from IoT devices, GPS systems, and digital twins—virtual representations of physical assets. These technologies provide continuous updates on the location, condition, and status of resources, enabling businesses to monitor their lifecycle stages effectively.

AI-powered predictive analytics further enhances tracking by forecasting resource movements and identifying potential bottlenecks or disruptions. For example, ML algorithms can predict delays in supply chain logistics, allowing organizations to take preemptive actions to maintain the flow of materials. This capability ensures that resources are delivered where they are needed, reducing inefficiencies and waste.

AI also supports the tracking of secondary materials, such as recycled or recovered resources. By monitoring their quality and availability, AI systems ensure that these materials are reintegrated into production cycles effectively. This capability aligns with CE principles by keeping resources in circulation and reducing reliance on virgin materials.

Applications Across Industries

AI-driven resource mapping and tracking have applications across various industries, each benefiting from improved efficiency and reduced waste:

- **Manufacturing:** AI tracks raw materials and components throughout the production process, ensuring optimal utilization and identifying waste points.
- **Retail:** AI monitors inventory levels and predicts restocking needs, reducing overstocking and waste.
- **Energy:** AI maps renewable energy resources, such as solar or wind, to optimize their use in energy grids.
- **Waste Management:** AI tracks recyclable materials from collection to processing, ensuring their recovery and reuse.

These applications demonstrate how AI enhances resource management by providing actionable insights that support CE objectives.

Overcoming Challenges

While AI offers significant advantages in resource mapping and tracking, its implementation is not without challenges. Issues such as data fragmentation, lack of interoperability between systems, and high implementation costs must be addressed to fully realize AI's potential. Additionally, ensuring data privacy and security is critical, as resource tracking often involves sensitive information.

Despite these challenges, the integration of AI into resource mapping and tracking is a transformative step toward achieving circularity. By providing real-time, accurate insights, AI empowers organizations to optimize resource use, reduce waste, and align their operations with CE principles.

Predictive Analytics for Demand Forecasting

Demand forecasting is a critical aspect of resource optimization in the CE, enabling businesses to anticipate material and product needs accurately. Predictive analytics, a key component of AI, transforms demand forecasting by analyzing historical and real-time data to identify patterns, trends, and relationships. This data-driven approach enhances decision-making, reduces waste, and aligns resource use with CE principles.

The Importance of Demand Forecasting

Demand forecasting helps businesses plan for the future by predicting customer demand for products and services. Accurate forecasts ensure that production aligns with demand, minimizing overproduction, underproduction, and resource wastage. In the context of CE, effective demand forecasting supports resource efficiency, reduces inventory waste, and enables circular business models such as leasing, sharing, and remanufacturing.

Traditional demand forecasting methods often rely on manual analysis or static models that fail to capture the complexity of modern markets. These methods are limited in their ability to respond to dynamic changes in consumer behavior, supply chain disruptions, or seasonal variations. Predictive analytics, powered by AI, addresses these limitations by providing real-time, adaptive insights that improve the accuracy and reliability of forecasts.

How Predictive Analytics Works

Predictive analytics uses ML algorithms and statistical models to process large volumes of data and generate forecasts. These algorithms analyze historical sales data, market trends, and external factors such as economic indicators or weather conditions to predict future demand patterns. By continuously learning from new data, predictive analytics adapts to changes in the market, ensuring that forecasts remain accurate over time.

One of the key strengths of predictive analytics is its ability to identify correlations and causations that are not immediately apparent. For example, it can detect how changes in consumer behavior during specific seasons or economic conditions impact demand for particular products. This granular understanding allows businesses to make informed decisions about production, inventory management, and resource allocation.

Applications in Resource Optimization

Predictive analytics for demand forecasting has numerous applications in optimizing resource use across industries:

- **Manufacturing:** AI-driven demand forecasts help manufacturers plan production schedules, ensuring that resources such as raw materials and labor are used efficiently. This reduces overproduction and minimizes waste.
- **Retail:** Retailers use predictive analytics to optimize inventory levels, avoiding stockouts or excess inventory that could lead to disposal.

- **Energy:** In the energy sector, predictive analytics forecasts electricity demand, enabling efficient grid management and optimal allocation of renewable energy resources.
- **Agriculture:** Farmers use predictive analytics to anticipate crop demand, reducing food waste and ensuring efficient use of water, fertilizers, and other inputs.

These applications demonstrate how predictive analytics enhances resource efficiency and supports CE principles by aligning supply with demand.

Improving Circular Business Models

Predictive analytics is also instrumental in enabling circular business models such as leasing, sharing, and product-as-a-service. By forecasting usage patterns and demand fluctuations, predictive analytics ensures optimal utilization of shared assets, reducing the need for additional production. For example, AI can predict the demand for shared vehicles in specific locations, allowing fleet operators to allocate resources efficiently.

In subscription-based models, predictive analytics helps businesses anticipate renewal rates and usage trends, enabling better inventory planning and customer retention strategies. This aligns with CE principles by promoting sustainable consumption and reducing resource consumption.

Challenges in Implementing Predictive Analytics

Despite its advantages, implementing predictive analytics for demand forecasting presents several challenges:

- **Data Quality and Availability:** Predictive models rely on high-quality, comprehensive data to generate accurate forecasts. Incomplete or inaccurate data can compromise their effectiveness.

- **Complexity and Cost:** Developing and deploying predictive analytics systems require significant investment in technology, expertise, and infrastructure, which may be prohibitive for smaller organizations.
- **Integration with Existing Systems:** Many businesses struggle to integrate predictive analytics with their current processes and supply chains, limiting its potential impact.

Addressing these challenges requires a combination of technological innovation, capacity building, and collaboration among stakeholders.

Future Opportunities

As predictive analytics technologies continue to evolve, their potential for demand forecasting in CE will expand. Advanced ML models, enhanced data collection methods, and greater integration with other AI-driven tools will further improve the accuracy and efficiency of demand forecasts. These advancements will empower businesses to optimize resource use, reduce waste, and fully embrace CE principles in their operations.

Machine Learning for Material Flow Optimization

Material flow optimization is a cornerstone of the CE, focusing on efficient management of resources as they move through production, distribution, usage, and recovery stages. ML, a subset of AI, has emerged as a transformative tool for optimizing these flows. By analyzing complex data, identifying inefficiencies, and predicting future patterns, ML enables organizations to enhance resource efficiency, reduce waste, and align operations with CE principles.

Understanding Material Flow Optimization

Material flow optimization involves managing the movement and transformation of materials within and across supply chains to minimize waste and maximize utility. This process includes monitoring raw materials, components, finished products, and end-of-life materials as they move through their lifecycle. Optimized material flows ensure that resources are used efficiently, remain in circulation for as long as possible, and are reintegrated into production cycles whenever possible.

In traditional systems, material flows are often managed manually or with static models that struggle to adapt to dynamic changes in supply chains. This results in inefficiencies such as overstocking, underutilization of resources, and waste generation. ML overcomes these limitations by leveraging data-driven insights and adaptive algorithms to optimize material flows in real time.

How Machine Learning Enhances Material Flow Optimization

ML enhances material flow optimization by processing vast amounts of data to identify patterns, trends, and inefficiencies. Unlike static models, ML algorithms continuously learn from new data, enabling them to adapt to changing conditions and improve their accuracy over time.

Demand Prediction

ML algorithms analyze historical sales data, market trends, and external factors to forecast demand for materials and products. Accurate demand predictions help organizations plan resource allocation, reduce overproduction, and minimize waste. This aligns with CE principles by ensuring that only the necessary resources are used, preventing excess materials from going to waste.

Inventory Management

ML enables real-time monitoring and optimization of inventory levels. By analyzing data on production rates, shipping schedules, and storage capacities, ML algorithms ensure that materials are available when needed without overstocking. This reduces storage costs, prevents spoilage, and minimizes the risk of materials becoming obsolete.

Production Scheduling

ML optimizes production schedules by analyzing factors such as machine availability, workforce capacity, and material supply. By aligning production processes with demand forecasts and resource availability, ML minimizes downtime, reduces resource consumption, and ensures efficient use of materials.

Waste Reduction

ML algorithms identify inefficiencies in production processes that lead to material waste. For example, they can detect patterns of overuse, defects, or bottlenecks that result in resource losses. By addressing these issues, organizations can reduce waste and improve overall efficiency.

End-of-Life Management

ML supports the recovery and recycling of materials by optimizing reverse logistics processes. Algorithms analyze data on returned products, recycling capacities, and transportation routes to ensure efficient collection and processing of end-of-life materials. This ensures that valuable resources are reintegrated into production cycles rather than being discarded.

Applications Across Industries

ML for material flow optimization has applications across a wide range of industries, each benefiting from improved resource efficiency and waste reduction:

- **Manufacturing:** ML optimizes material flows within factories by monitoring production lines, identifying inefficiencies, and ensuring timely delivery of raw materials. This reduces downtime, enhances productivity, and minimizes waste.

- **Retail:** Retailers use ML to optimize inventory levels, ensuring that products are stocked appropriately to meet demand without overproduction. This reduces storage costs and prevents unsold items from being wasted.
- **Logistics:** ML optimizes transportation routes and schedules, reducing fuel consumption and ensuring timely delivery of materials. By minimizing transportation inefficiencies, ML contributes to lower emissions and improved resource efficiency.
- **Waste Management:** ML supports efficient sorting and recycling of materials by analyzing data on waste streams and recycling capacities. This ensures that materials are recovered and reintegrated into production cycles effectively.

Challenges in Implementing Machine Learning

While ML offers significant benefits for material flow optimization, its implementation is not without challenges:

- **Data Availability and Quality:** ML relies on large volumes of accurate, high-quality data to generate insights. Inconsistent or incomplete data can compromise the effectiveness of ML algorithms.
- **Integration with Existing Systems:** Many organizations face difficulties integrating ML solutions with their existing supply chain and production systems. This requires significant investment in technology and expertise.
- **Cost of Implementation:** Developing and deploying ML solutions involves upfront costs for software, hardware, and skilled personnel. For SMEs, these costs may be prohibitive.
- **Ethical and Privacy Concerns:** The use of ML in material flow optimization raises ethical issues related to data privacy and security. Organizations must ensure that data is collected and used responsibly to avoid breaches and maintain stakeholder trust.

Future Directions

As ML technologies continue to advance, their potential for material flow optimization will expand. Emerging techniques such as reinforcement learning and advanced neural networks promise to enhance the accuracy and efficiency of ML algorithms. Additionally, greater integration with other AI-driven tools, such as predictive analytics and IoT devices, will further improve the ability of ML to optimize material flows.

Through these advancements, ML will play an increasingly important role in enabling organizations to achieve circularity, reduce waste, and maximize resource efficiency. By addressing the challenges of implementation and scaling, businesses can unlock the full potential of ML for material flow optimization in the CE.

Challenges and Limitations in AI-Driven Resource Optimization

AI holds immense potential for optimizing resources in alignment with CE principles. However, its application is not without challenges and limitations. The integration of AI into resource optimization faces technological, economic, and organizational hurdles that must be addressed to fully realize its potential.

Data-Related Challenges

Data serves as the backbone of AI-driven resource optimization. However, the availability, quality, and accessibility of data pose significant challenges:

- **Data Availability:** Many industries lack the necessary data infrastructure to support AI applications. Resource optimization requires detailed information on material flows, production processes, and waste streams, which may not be readily available or consistently collected.

- **Data Quality:** Poor data quality, including inaccuracies, inconsistencies, and outdated records, undermines the effectiveness of AI algorithms. Incomplete or fragmented datasets can lead to flawed insights and suboptimal decision-making.
- **Data Integration:** Integrating data from diverse sources, such as supply chains, IoT devices, and production systems, is a complex task. Variations in data formats, standards, and systems create barriers to seamless data consolidation and analysis.

Technological Limitations

While AI technologies have advanced significantly, certain technological limitations hinder their application in resource optimization:

- **Algorithm Complexity:** Developing AI algorithms that can accurately model complex resource flows and predict optimization scenarios requires significant expertise. These algorithms must account for numerous variables and uncertainties, which increases their complexity and computational demands.
- **Infrastructure Requirements:** AI applications require robust digital infrastructure, including high-speed connectivity, advanced computing power, and sensor networks. Many organizations, especially in developing regions, lack access to such infrastructure, limiting their ability to adopt AI-driven solutions.
- **Real-Time Processing:** Resource optimization often requires real-time analysis and decision-making. AI systems capable of processing and responding to data in real time can be expensive and technically challenging to implement.

Economic Barriers

The cost of developing, implementing, and maintaining AI systems poses a significant challenge for many organizations:

- **High Initial Costs:** AI solutions involve substantial upfront investment in technology, infrastructure, and skilled personnel. SMEs may struggle to allocate resources for these expenses.
- **Uncertain Return on Investment (ROI):** The benefits of AI-driven resource optimization, such as cost savings and waste reduction, are often realized over the long term. This delayed ROI can discourage businesses from adopting AI solutions, especially in industries with tight profit margins.
- **Scalability Issues:** Scaling AI solutions across multiple operations, facilities, or regions can be cost-intensive and logistically complex, further limiting their adoption.

Organizational and Cultural Challenges

AI-driven resource optimization requires significant changes to organizational structures, processes, and mindsets, which can encounter resistance:

- **Lack of Expertise:** Implementing AI solutions requires expertise in data science, ML, and resource management. Many organizations lack the necessary skills and struggle to recruit or train personnel with the required capabilities.
- **Resistance to Change:** Employees and stakeholders accustomed to traditional resource management methods may resist adopting AI-driven approaches. Overcoming this inertia requires extensive education, training, and demonstration of AI's benefits.
- **Integration with Existing Processes:** AI solutions must be integrated into existing workflows and systems, which can disrupt established processes. This integration often requires reengineering operations, which may be time-consuming and resource-intensive.

Ethical and Regulatory Concerns

The application of AI in resource optimization raises ethical and regulatory issues that need to be addressed.

- **Data Privacy:** Resource optimization often involves collecting and analyzing sensitive data from supply chains, production systems, and consumers. Ensuring data privacy and security is critical to maintaining trust and compliance with regulations.
- **Algorithmic Bias:** AI algorithms may inadvertently reflect biases present in the data they are trained on, leading to unequal or unfair outcomes. Addressing these biases requires careful algorithm design and continuous monitoring.
- **Regulatory Uncertainty:** The evolving nature of AI and CE regulations creates uncertainty for businesses. Inconsistent policies across regions further complicate the deployment of AI solutions on a global scale.

Future Considerations

Overcoming these challenges and limitations requires a coordinated effort among businesses, governments, and technology providers. Investments in data infrastructure, advancements in AI technologies, and policies that promote equitable access and innovation are essential for unlocking the full potential of AI-driven resource optimization. By addressing these barriers, organizations can harness AI to drive efficiency, reduce waste, and support the transition to a CE.

Chapter 3: AI for Waste Minimization

Waste minimization is a cornerstone of the CE, focusing on reducing material losses and environmental impact across production, consumption, and disposal stages. AI offers powerful tools to revolutionize waste management by identifying inefficiencies, optimizing resource recovery, and enhancing recycling processes. This chapter explores the transformative role of AI in minimizing waste, from advanced material identification and sorting systems to predictive analytics for reducing production waste. By examining these applications, this chapter demonstrates how AI enables industries to align with CE principles and move closer to achieving zero-waste systems.

AI Applications in Waste Identification and Classification

Waste identification and classification are critical steps in waste minimization and resource recovery within the CE. Efficiently separating materials for recycling, reusing, or safe disposal ensures that resources remain in circulation and environmental harm is minimized. AI has emerged as a transformative technology in this domain, offering advanced capabilities for automating and enhancing the accuracy of waste identification and classification processes.

The Importance of Waste Identification and Classification

Effective waste management begins with accurately identifying and classifying materials. This involves determining the type, quality, and condition of waste items, which directly impacts their recyclability and the efficiency of resource recovery processes. Traditional methods of waste identification often rely on manual sorting, which is labor-intensive, error-prone, and inefficient. Misclassification of materials can lead to contamination in recycling streams, reduced recovery rates, and increased waste sent to landfills.

41

AI addresses these challenges by automating waste identification and classification, providing precise and scalable solutions that improve the efficiency and effectiveness of waste management systems. Through ML, computer vision, and data analytics, AI enables real-time recognition and sorting of waste, ensuring that valuable materials are recovered and reused.

AI-Powered Computer Vision for Waste Identification

Computer vision, a subset of AI, plays a central role in waste identification. By analyzing visual data captured by cameras or sensors, computer vision systems can detect and classify waste items based on their physical characteristics, such as shape, color, texture, and size. This technology enables automated sorting systems to differentiate between various materials, including plastics, metals, paper, and glass.

For example, AI algorithms trained on large datasets of labeled waste images can identify different types of plastics, such as polyethylene terephthalate (PET) and high-density polyethylene (HDPE), with high accuracy. These systems can also detect contamination, such as food residue or mixed materials, which might affect recyclability. By improving the precision of waste identification, AI reduces contamination rates and enhances the quality of recovered materials.

Machine Learning for Classification Optimization

ML enhances the classification process by continuously learning and adapting to new data. ML algorithms analyze patterns in waste characteristics and sorting outcomes, refining their ability to classify materials over time. This adaptability ensures that AI systems remain effective even as waste composition changes due to shifts in consumer behavior or product design.

ML also enables predictive analytics, which helps waste management facilities anticipate changes in waste streams and optimize their operations accordingly. For example, predictive models can forecast the volume and type of waste generated during specific periods, such as holiday seasons or product launches, allowing facilities to allocate resources more efficiently.

Real-Time Sorting Systems

AI-powered waste identification and classification systems are increasingly being integrated into real-time sorting processes in recycling facilities. These systems use conveyor belts equipped with cameras and sensors that capture data on waste items as they move through the sorting line. AI algorithms process this data instantaneously, directing robotic arms or air jets to separate materials into appropriate categories.

Real-time sorting systems improve the speed and accuracy of waste processing, reducing reliance on manual labor and increasing throughput. They also enable the recovery of materials that might otherwise be missed by human operators, such as small or irregularly shaped items. This ensures that more materials are diverted from landfills and reintroduced into production cycles.

Applications Across Industries

AI applications in waste identification and classification are not limited to recycling facilities. They are also being adopted in various industries to enhance waste management practices:

- **Manufacturing:** AI systems identify and separate production waste, such as defective components or offcuts, ensuring that recyclable materials are recovered.
- **Retail:** Retailers use AI to classify packaging waste, enabling more efficient recycling and compliance with waste management regulations.
- **Construction:** AI-powered solutions identify construction and demolition waste, such as concrete, wood, and metals, for reuse or recycling.

- **Healthcare:** In medical facilities, AI systems classify biomedical waste to ensure proper handling and disposal, minimizing environmental risks.

Challenges and Future Directions

Despite its potential, the implementation of AI in waste identification and classification faces challenges. High upfront costs for AI systems, limited access to labeled datasets for training algorithms, and the need for robust infrastructure can be barriers to adoption. Additionally, integrating AI systems with existing waste management processes requires significant investment and expertise.

As technology advances, AI applications in waste management are expected to become more accessible and cost-effective. Emerging innovations, such as hybrid AI models and advanced sensor technologies, promise to further enhance the precision and scalability of waste identification and classification systems. By overcoming these challenges, AI has the potential to transform waste management practices, ensuring more efficient resource recovery and supporting the goals of the CE.

Role of AI in Designing Waste-Free Manufacturing Processes

AI is revolutionizing the manufacturing industry by enabling the design and implementation of waste-free processes. Through advanced analytics, ML, and automation, AI provides manufacturers with the tools to optimize resource use, minimize waste generation, and align production systems with the principles of the CE. These innovations reduce environmental impact, improve operational efficiency, and enhance the sustainability of manufacturing practices.

Understanding Waste-Free Manufacturing

Waste-free manufacturing refers to the creation of processes and systems that minimize material and energy waste at every stage of production. This involves efficient use of raw materials, reduction of defective products, and recovery or recycling of byproducts. Achieving waste-free manufacturing is critical for transitioning from traditional linear production models to circular systems that prioritize resource efficiency and sustainability.

AI plays a central role in this transition by addressing inefficiencies in manufacturing processes and enabling real-time optimization. By leveraging data and advanced algorithms, AI helps manufacturers identify waste sources, improve design and production techniques, and implement closed-loop systems that reduce reliance on virgin resources.

AI-Powered Process Optimization

AI optimizes manufacturing processes by analyzing data from production lines to identify inefficiencies and areas for improvement. ML algorithms process data from sensors, IoT devices, and enterprise systems to detect patterns and correlations that human operators might overlook. These insights enable manufacturers to make data-driven decisions that reduce waste and improve resource utilization.

Material Optimization

AI helps manufacturers optimize material use by analyzing production data to determine the exact quantities of raw materials needed for specific products. This reduces excess material usage and prevents overproduction. AI can also recommend alternative materials that are more sustainable or easier to recycle, further reducing waste.

Energy Efficiency

By monitoring energy consumption in real time, AI identifies inefficiencies in energy use across production systems. Predictive analytics can forecast energy needs and optimize operations to reduce energy waste, lowering costs and environmental impact.

Minimizing Defects

AI systems detect defects in products early in the production process, preventing defective items from reaching later stages or being discarded. Computer vision technologies, combined with ML, inspect products for flaws with high precision, ensuring quality while minimizing waste.

Generative Design for Waste Reduction

Generative design, powered by AI, is a transformative approach to creating products and manufacturing processes that inherently minimize waste. This technique uses algorithms to generate multiple design options based on specified parameters such as material use, durability, and environmental impact.

Product Design

AI-driven generative design allows engineers to create products that use fewer materials, are modular, and are easier to repair or recycle. These designs align with CE principles by ensuring that products have a longer lifespan and minimal environmental footprint.

Process Design

Generative design also applies to manufacturing processes, enabling the creation of workflows that minimize waste and optimize resource use. By simulating different scenarios, AI identifies the most efficient production methods and eliminates unnecessary steps or materials.

Predictive Maintenance and Waste Prevention

AI enhances waste-free manufacturing by enabling predictive maintenance, which reduces downtime and prevents unnecessary waste of resources. By analyzing data from machinery and equipment, AI systems predict when maintenance is required, avoiding unexpected breakdowns that lead to production delays and material losses.

Predictive maintenance also extends the lifespan of manufacturing equipment, reducing the need for frequent replacements and associated resource consumption. This contributes to overall resource efficiency and waste reduction in manufacturing systems.

Closed-Loop Systems and Byproduct Recovery

AI facilitates the implementation of closed-loop manufacturing systems, where waste materials are recovered and reintegrated into production cycles. ML algorithms analyze byproducts generated during manufacturing to determine their potential for reuse or recycling.

For example, AI can identify ways to repurpose scrap materials or optimize recycling processes to recover valuable components. This ensures that resources remain in circulation and reduces the reliance on virgin materials, aligning with CE goals.

Applications Across Industries

AI-driven waste-free manufacturing processes are being adopted across a range of industries:

- **Automotive:** AI optimizes material use in vehicle production, reduces scrap, and enhances recycling of end-of-life vehicles.

- **Electronics:** AI designs modular and repairable devices, enabling easier recovery of valuable components and materials.
- **Textiles:** AI minimizes fabric waste in apparel production by optimizing cutting patterns and recycling textile byproducts.
- **Pharmaceuticals:** AI enhances precision in drug manufacturing, reducing waste from overproduction or defective batches.

Challenges and Future Directions

Despite its potential, the adoption of AI in waste-free manufacturing faces challenges such as high implementation costs, data integration issues, and the need for skilled personnel. Additionally, SMEs may lack the resources to invest in AI technologies.

As AI technologies advance, they will become more accessible and cost-effective, enabling broader adoption across the manufacturing sector. Innovations in areas such as real-time data analytics, advanced robotics, and digital twins will further enhance the ability of AI to design and implement waste-free manufacturing processes. By addressing these challenges, manufacturers can fully leverage AI to achieve sustainability goals and support the transition to a CE.

Optimizing Recycling and Re-Manufacturing with AI

AI is transforming recycling and re-manufacturing processes, enabling more efficient recovery and reuse of materials. These technologies are critical for the CE, where maintaining resources in circulation is a central goal. By leveraging ML, computer vision, robotics, and predictive analytics, AI enhances the precision, scalability, and cost-effectiveness of recycling and re-manufacturing operations. This reduces waste, lowers environmental impacts, and promotes sustainable resource use.

The Importance of Recycling and Re-Manufacturing in the Circular Economy

Recycling and re-manufacturing are essential components of CE, as they enable the recovery of valuable materials and products at the end of their lifecycle. Recycling focuses on breaking down materials to create raw inputs for new products, while re-manufacturing involves restoring used items to a like-new condition for reuse. Together, these processes reduce the demand for virgin materials, minimize waste, and extend the lifecycle of resources.

Despite their benefits, traditional recycling and re-manufacturing systems often face challenges such as inefficiencies in material separation, contamination in recycling streams, and limitations in product recovery. AI addresses these issues by automating and optimizing processes, ensuring that resources are recovered effectively and reintroduced into production cycles.

AI-Driven Material Identification and Sorting

One of the most significant contributions of AI to recycling is its ability to accurately identify and sort materials. Computer vision systems, powered by ML algorithms, analyze visual data from sensors and cameras to detect and classify materials based on their physical properties, such as color, shape, and texture. These systems can distinguish between various types of plastics, metals, glass, and paper, even in complex waste streams.

AI-powered sorting systems are integrated into recycling facilities, where robotic arms or air jets separate materials in real time based on the classifications provided by AI. This level of precision reduces contamination in recycling streams and ensures that high-quality materials are recovered for reuse. For example, AI can differentiate between PET and HDPE plastics, ensuring that each type is processed correctly and meets the standards required for re-manufacturing.

Enhancing Process Efficiency with Machine Learning

ML algorithms optimize recycling and re-manufacturing processes by analyzing operational data and identifying inefficiencies. These algorithms continuously learn from new data, allowing facilities to improve performance over time.

Predictive Maintenance

AI systems monitor equipment in recycling and re-manufacturing facilities, predicting maintenance needs to prevent unexpected breakdowns. This reduces downtime and ensures that processes run smoothly, maximizing throughput and minimizing waste.

Energy Optimization

Recycling and re-manufacturing processes often consume significant amounts of energy. AI analyzes energy usage patterns and identifies opportunities to reduce consumption without compromising efficiency, lowering operational costs and environmental impact.

Waste Reduction

AI identifies points in the process where material losses occur, such as during shredding, melting, or reassembly. By addressing these inefficiencies, facilities can recover more materials and reduce the volume of waste generated.

AI in Closed-Loop Manufacturing

AI plays a pivotal role in supporting closed-loop manufacturing systems, where recycled materials are reintegrated into production cycles. Predictive analytics and advanced algorithms ensure that recovered materials meet the quality standards required for manufacturing new products. This includes detecting impurities or defects that could compromise the performance of the final product.

For example, in the automotive industry, AI systems analyze recovered metals to ensure they meet the specifications needed for producing vehicle components. In electronics, AI optimizes the recovery of rare earth elements from discarded devices, enabling their reuse in manufacturing.

Re-Manufacturing with AI-Driven Precision

Re-manufacturing involves restoring used products to a like-new condition, which often requires disassembly, cleaning, repair, and reassembly. AI enhances each stage of this process:

- **Disassembly:** AI-powered robotics systems automate the disassembly of complex products, such as electronics or machinery, with high precision. This reduces labor costs and ensures that components are not damaged during the process.
- **Quality Inspection:** Computer vision systems inspect components for wear and defects, ensuring that only parts suitable for reuse are reintegrated into products. ML algorithms assess inspection data to identify trends and recommend process improvements.
- **Reassembly Optimization:** AI analyzes reassembly processes to optimize workflows, reducing the time and resources required to restore products. This enhances the scalability and cost-effectiveness of re-manufacturing operations.

Applications Across Industries

AI-driven recycling and re-manufacturing technologies are being adopted across various industries:

- **Electronics:** AI systems recover valuable metals, such as gold and cobalt, from discarded devices while ensuring compliance with e-waste regulations.

- **Automotive:** AI optimizes the recycling of metals and the re-manufacturing of components such as engines and transmissions.
- **Textiles:** AI-powered systems sort and recycle fabrics, enabling the production of new garments from post-consumer waste.
- **Construction:** AI facilitates the recovery of materials such as concrete, steel, and wood from demolition waste for reuse in new projects.

Challenges and Future Directions

While AI offers significant advantages for recycling and re-manufacturing, its implementation is not without challenges. High initial costs, the need for specialized expertise, and the integration of AI systems with existing processes can be barriers to adoption. Additionally, ensuring the quality and availability of data for training AI algorithms is critical for achieving accurate and reliable results.

As technology advances, AI-driven solutions for recycling and re-manufacturing will become more accessible and efficient. Emerging innovations, such as digital twins and advanced robotics, promise to further enhance these processes, enabling industries to recover more resources and reduce waste. By addressing current challenges and leveraging AI's potential, organizations can build more sustainable systems that align with the goals of the CE.

AI's Role in Supporting a Zero-Waste Future

AI plays a transformative role in achieving a zero-waste future by optimizing resource use, minimizing waste generation, and enhancing material recovery processes. By integrating advanced technologies such as ML, predictive analytics, and robotics, AI enables industries, governments, and consumers to adopt practices that align with the principles of a CE. These innovations drive efficiency, reduce environmental impact, and pave the way for sustainable systems that prioritize waste prevention and resource circularity.

Optimizing Resource Use

AI enhances resource efficiency by identifying areas of inefficiency and recommending improvements across supply chains and production processes. ML algorithms analyze data from production systems to optimize material use, ensuring that resources are allocated precisely where needed. This reduces excess consumption and prevents overproduction, which are significant contributors to waste.

In industries such as manufacturing, AI-powered systems monitor raw material inputs and production outputs to minimize resource losses. Predictive analytics forecasts demand with high accuracy, enabling businesses to align production levels with actual needs and avoid unnecessary waste. AI also identifies opportunities to substitute resource-intensive materials with sustainable alternatives, further supporting waste reduction.

Reducing Waste at the Design Stage

AI plays a critical role in designing products and systems that generate minimal waste. Generative design tools, powered by AI, allow engineers to create products that are modular, durable, and easily repairable or recyclable. By analyzing millions of design permutations, AI identifies configurations that use the least amount of material while maintaining product performance.

AI-driven design tools also support lifecycle analysis, enabling manufacturers to assess the environmental impact of a product from production to disposal. This holistic approach ensures that waste prevention is considered at every stage of the product's lifecycle, aligning with the goals of zero-waste systems.

Enhancing Recycling and Resource Recovery

Recycling is a cornerstone of a zero-waste future, and AI significantly enhances its efficiency and scalability. AI-powered computer vision systems identify and sort materials with precision, reducing contamination in recycling streams and improving the quality of recovered materials. ML algorithms continuously refine these systems, ensuring that they adapt to changes in waste composition over time.

Robotics, integrated with AI, automates the sorting and separation of materials in recycling facilities. These systems can handle high volumes of waste with speed and accuracy, reducing reliance on manual labor and increasing throughput. AI also supports the recovery of rare and valuable materials, such as rare earth elements from electronics, by optimizing separation processes and minimizing losses.

Supporting Circular Supply Chains

AI enables the creation of circular supply chains, where materials are kept in continuous circulation rather than being discarded as waste. Predictive analytics tracks material flows and identifies opportunities for reuse, repair, and remanufacturing. This ensures that resources are reintegrated into production cycles, reducing the demand for virgin materials.

In addition, AI enhances reverse logistics, the process of returning products and materials from consumers to manufacturers. By analyzing data on transportation routes, consumer behavior, and product conditions, AI optimizes the collection and redistribution of materials, ensuring that they are processed efficiently and effectively.

Empowering Waste Prevention at the Consumer Level

AI-driven tools empower consumers to make sustainable choices that reduce waste. Smart apps and platforms use AI to provide personalized recommendations for waste prevention, such as suggesting reusable alternatives to single-use products or identifying nearby recycling facilities. These tools also educate consumers on proper waste disposal practices, reducing contamination in recycling streams.

In smart cities, AI-powered waste management systems analyze data from IoT sensors to optimize waste collection schedules and routes. This reduces the frequency of waste pickups, conserves fuel, and minimizes emissions, contributing to a more sustainable urban environment.

Addressing Challenges in Achieving Zero-Waste

Despite its potential, the integration of AI into zero-waste initiatives faces challenges such as high implementation costs, data accessibility issues, and the need for technical expertise. Ensuring the scalability of AI-driven solutions across regions and industries requires significant investment in infrastructure and capacity building.

Ethical considerations, such as data privacy and the equitable distribution of AI benefits, must also be addressed. Inclusive policies and frameworks are essential to ensure that AI technologies support sustainable development without exacerbating social inequalities.

Future Opportunities

As AI technologies continue to advance, their role in supporting a zero-waste future will expand. Innovations such as blockchain-integrated AI for supply chain transparency, advanced robotics for material recovery, and real-time data analytics for waste monitoring will further enhance the ability of industries and governments to prevent waste and promote circularity. By leveraging these advancements, stakeholders can accelerate the transition to a zero-waste future and create systems that prioritize sustainability and resilience.

Chapter 4: AI in Sustainable Product Design

Sustainable product design is a crucial element of the CE, ensuring that products are created to minimize environmental impact throughout their lifecycle. AI is revolutionizing this process by enabling innovative approaches to material selection, modularity, durability, and recyclability. This chapter explores how AI-driven tools, such as generative design, predictive analytics, and lifecycle assessment technologies, empower designers and manufacturers to develop products that align with sustainability goals. By examining these applications, the chapter highlights AI's role in shaping a future where products are optimized for resource efficiency, longevity, and minimal waste.

Role of AI in Lifecycle Analysis and Design Innovation

AI is revolutionizing lifecycle analysis (LCA) and design innovation by enabling more accurate assessments of environmental impact and fostering the creation of sustainable products. These advancements are critical for aligning with the principles of the CE, as they support resource efficiency, waste minimization, and long-term sustainability. By integrating AI into LCA and design processes, businesses can make informed decisions that reduce environmental impact while driving innovation.

Understanding Lifecycle Analysis

Lifecycle analysis is a systematic approach to evaluating the environmental impact of a product across its entire lifecycle, from raw material extraction to end-of-life disposal or recycling. This includes assessing energy consumption, greenhouse gas emissions, water use, and waste generation at every stage. LCA provides valuable insights for identifying opportunities to improve sustainability and reduce the environmental footprint of products.

Traditional LCA methods often rely on manual data collection and static models, which can be time-consuming and prone to errors. AI enhances LCA by automating data analysis, improving accuracy, and providing real-time insights. ML algorithms, big data analytics, and predictive models enable comprehensive assessments that are more precise and scalable than traditional approaches.

AI-Driven Enhancements in Lifecycle Analysis

1. Data Collection and Integration:

AI streamlines data collection by integrating information from diverse sources, such as IoT devices, production databases, and environmental monitoring systems. ML algorithms process large datasets to identify patterns and correlations that inform lifecycle assessments. This ensures that all relevant factors are considered, providing a holistic view of a product's environmental impact.

2. Real-Time Monitoring:

AI enables real-time monitoring of environmental impact throughout a product's lifecycle. Sensors and AI-powered analytics track energy use, emissions, and material consumption during production and use phases. These real-time insights allow manufacturers to address inefficiencies and reduce environmental impact proactively.

3. Scenario Modeling:

AI supports scenario modeling by simulating different design, production, and disposal scenarios to evaluate their environmental implications. Predictive analytics helps manufacturers identify the most sustainable options, optimizing resource use and minimizing waste.

AI's Role in Design Innovation

Design innovation focuses on creating products that are functional, durable, and sustainable. AI plays a transformative role in this process by enabling generative design, material optimization, and modularity, all of which are essential for advancing CE principles.

Generative Design

AI-driven generative design tools use algorithms to explore countless design options based on predefined parameters such as material efficiency, durability, and recyclability. These tools suggest innovative designs that use fewer resources while maintaining or enhancing product performance. For example, generative design can reduce material waste by optimizing structural components for strength and efficiency.

Material Selection

AI assists in selecting sustainable materials by analyzing material properties, availability, and environmental impact. ML algorithms identify alternatives to resource-intensive or non-recyclable materials, ensuring that products align with CE goals. AI can also evaluate the recyclability and biodegradability of materials, further supporting sustainable design.

Modularity and Repairability

AI enables the design of modular products that are easy to repair, upgrade, or disassemble for recycling. By analyzing product usage patterns and failure rates, AI provides insights into how products can be designed for longer lifespans and easier maintenance. This reduces waste and extends the usability of resources.

Applications Across Industries

AI's role in LCA and design innovation spans various industries, each benefiting from enhanced sustainability and efficiency:

- **Automotive:** AI optimizes vehicle design for lightweight materials and fuel efficiency, reducing emissions and energy use.
- **Electronics:** AI supports modular design in consumer electronics, enabling easier upgrades and recycling.
- **Textiles:** AI analyzes lifecycle data to promote sustainable fabric choices and waste reduction in fashion design.
- **Construction:** AI evaluates the lifecycle impact of building materials, optimizing designs for energy efficiency and recyclability.

Challenges and Future Directions

Despite its advantages, the integration of AI into LCA and design innovation faces challenges such as high implementation costs, data fragmentation, and a lack of standardized metrics. Ensuring accessibility and scalability of AI-driven solutions will be essential for broader adoption across industries.

As technology advances, AI will play an increasingly central role in shaping sustainable design practices. Emerging innovations, such as advanced digital twins and blockchain-integrated data, promise to enhance LCA accuracy and foster greater collaboration among stakeholders. By leveraging these advancements, businesses can drive design innovation that supports CE principles and builds a more sustainable future.

Using AI for Material Selection and Product Modularity

AI has become a transformative tool in advancing material selection and product modularity, two essential aspects of sustainable product design in the CE. By leveraging ML, data analytics, and predictive modeling, AI enables manufacturers to identify optimal materials for sustainability and durability while designing modular products that are easier to repair, upgrade, and recycle. These capabilities align with CE principles by reducing resource consumption, minimizing waste, and extending product lifespans.

AI in Material Selection

Material selection is a critical factor in designing sustainable products, as it determines a product's durability, environmental impact, and recyclability. AI enhances material selection by analyzing extensive datasets, such as material properties, environmental impact assessments, and lifecycle data, to identify the most suitable options.

Analyzing Material Properties

AI-driven tools process data on material properties, such as strength, flexibility, heat resistance, and chemical composition, to recommend the best materials for specific applications. ML algorithms evaluate trade-offs between performance and sustainability, ensuring that selected materials meet functional requirements while minimizing environmental impact.

Promoting Sustainable Alternatives

AI identifies sustainable material alternatives by analyzing environmental impact data. For example, AI can suggest biodegradable or recyclable materials instead of single-use plastics, reducing the environmental footprint of products. It can also analyze the availability of recycled materials, promoting their use in new products and reducing dependence on virgin resources.

Lifecycle Considerations

AI integrates lifecycle data into material selection processes, evaluating the environmental impact of materials from extraction to end-of-life. This holistic approach ensures that selected materials align with CE goals, such as reducing greenhouse gas emissions, conserving energy, and enhancing recyclability.

Cost Efficiency and Availability

AI systems analyze market trends and supply chain data to ensure that selected materials are not only sustainable but also cost-effective and readily available. This capability helps manufacturers balance sustainability objectives with economic considerations.

AI in Product Modularity

Product modularity involves designing products with interchangeable components that can be easily repaired, upgraded, or recycled. This approach reduces waste, extends product lifespans, and facilitates resource recovery. AI plays a key role in enabling modular design by providing insights into usage patterns, failure rates, and design optimization.

Design Optimization for Modularity

AI-powered generative design tools explore numerous design configurations to create modular products. These tools ensure that components are easily detachable, reducing the complexity of repairs and upgrades. For instance, AI can optimize the placement of screws or connectors to simplify disassembly without compromising product durability.

Predicting Component Lifespan

AI analyzes usage data to predict the lifespan of individual components. This insight allows manufacturers to design modular products that prioritize replaceable or upgradable parts, ensuring that products remain functional and relevant for longer periods.

Customizing Modular Designs

AI enables the customization of modular products to meet diverse consumer needs. By analyzing customer preferences and market trends, AI-driven tools suggest modular configurations that maximize user satisfaction while reducing resource consumption. This approach promotes the adoption of sustainable consumption patterns.

Facilitating End-of-Life Management

Modular products are easier to disassemble and recycle, aligning with CE principles. AI enhances this process by providing detailed data on material composition and component interconnectivity, streamlining recycling and material recovery efforts.

Applications Across Industries

AI-driven material selection and modular design are being adopted across various industries to advance sustainability:

- **Electronics:** AI optimizes modular designs for smartphones, laptops, and other consumer electronics, allowing users to replace or upgrade components instead of discarding entire devices.
- **Automotive:** AI supports the use of lightweight, sustainable materials in vehicle design and promotes modular components for easier repairs and upgrades.
- **Furniture:** Modular furniture designs benefit from AI's ability to analyze material properties and suggest configurations that enhance durability and recyclability.
- **Apparel:** AI facilitates material selection in the fashion industry, promoting the use of sustainable textiles and modular designs for reusable or repairable clothing items.

Challenges and Future Directions

Despite its potential, the integration of AI into material selection and modular design faces challenges such as limited access to comprehensive material datasets, high implementation costs, and resistance to change within industries. Overcoming these barriers requires investments in technology, education, and collaboration among stakeholders.

As AI technologies continue to evolve, their applications in material selection and modularity will expand. Innovations such as blockchain-integrated AI for tracking material provenance and advanced generative design algorithms promise to further enhance the sustainability of products. By leveraging these advancements, manufacturers can create products that support CE objectives, reduce waste, and foster a more sustainable future.

Generative Design Tools and Their Impact on Sustainability

Generative design tools, powered by AI, are transforming the field of product development by enabling innovative, efficient, and sustainable solutions. These tools use algorithms to explore a vast number of design permutations based on specific criteria, such as material efficiency, structural integrity, and environmental impact. By optimizing designs to reduce resource use and waste, generative design aligns with the principles of the CE and contributes significantly to sustainability goals.

How Generative Design Tools Work

Generative design tools use AI algorithms to create multiple design options from a set of predefined parameters. These parameters can include physical constraints, performance requirements, cost limits, material choices, and environmental considerations. Unlike traditional design methods, where engineers manually create and test concepts, generative design automates this process, enabling the rapid exploration of a broader range of solutions.

Data Input

The process begins with engineers inputting parameters into the generative design software. These inputs can include material properties, load requirements, production methods, and sustainability goals.

Algorithmic Exploration

AI algorithms generate thousands or even millions of design options that meet the input criteria. Each iteration is analyzed for performance, efficiency, and feasibility, allowing engineers to identify optimal solutions.

Evaluation and Selection

Designers evaluate the generated options based on key performance indicators (KPIs) such as material use, weight reduction, cost efficiency, and environmental impact. The most suitable design is then selected for prototyping and production.

Feedback and Iteration

Generative design tools allow for continuous refinement. Feedback from prototypes or simulations can be fed back into the system, enabling further optimization.

Applications of Generative Design in Sustainability

Generative design tools are driving sustainability across industries by optimizing material use, reducing waste, and enhancing the recyclability of products. Key applications include:

- **Material Efficiency:** Generative design minimizes material use by creating lightweight structures that maintain strength and durability. For example, in automotive and aerospace industries, these tools design components that are lighter and use fewer resources, reducing material costs and fuel consumption.

- **Waste Reduction:** By optimizing manufacturing processes, generative design reduces waste during production. Designs are tailored for additive manufacturing (3D printing), which generates minimal waste compared to traditional subtractive methods. This approach is particularly valuable for industries aiming to minimize resource wastage.
- **Recyclability and Modularity:** Generative design incorporates recyclability and modularity into product development. By analyzing material properties and assembly processes, these tools create designs that are easier to disassemble and recycle, supporting CE principles.
- **Energy Efficiency:** Generative design optimizes product geometry for energy efficiency. For example, in building design, generative tools create structures that maximize natural lighting and ventilation, reducing reliance on artificial lighting and climate control systems.
- **Cost Optimization:** Sustainability and cost-effectiveness often go hand in hand. Generative design identifies solutions that reduce material and production costs while achieving environmental goals, making sustainable products economically viable.

Impact Across Industries

Generative design is having a profound impact on sustainability efforts in various sectors:

- **Automotive and Aerospace:** Generative design tools are used to create lightweight components that reduce vehicle weight, improve fuel efficiency, and lower emissions. For example, AI-driven designs have enabled automakers to reduce the material used in engine mounts and suspension systems without compromising performance.

- **Construction and Architecture:** In the construction industry, generative design optimizes the use of sustainable materials and creates energy-efficient building layouts. These tools also enhance structural integrity while reducing material consumption, contributing to greener building practices.
- **Consumer Electronics:** Generative design improves the sustainability of electronic devices by reducing material use and simplifying assembly processes. Modular designs created with AI tools make devices easier to repair, upgrade, and recycle, extending product lifespans.
- **Healthcare:** In medical device design, generative tools optimize the use of biocompatible materials and create lightweight, patient-specific implants. These innovations reduce waste and improve patient outcomes.
- **Apparel and Fashion:** The fashion industry leverages generative design to optimize fabric cutting patterns, minimizing textile waste during production. These tools also promote the use of sustainable materials in clothing design.

Challenges and Limitations

While generative design offers significant sustainability benefits, its adoption faces challenges:

- **High Initial Costs:** Implementing generative design requires investment in software, hardware, and training. These costs can be a barrier for SMEs.
- **Integration with Existing Processes:** Adopting generative design tools often requires rethinking traditional design and production workflows. Integrating these tools into legacy systems can be complex and resource-intensive.
- **Data Dependency:** Generative design relies heavily on accurate data inputs. Incomplete or low-quality data can compromise the effectiveness of AI algorithms and lead to suboptimal results.

- **Design Interpretation:** The unconventional designs generated by AI tools may challenge traditional manufacturing methods or require new production techniques, such as 3D printing, which may not be widely available.

Future Opportunities

As AI technologies continue to advance, generative design tools will become more accessible and sophisticated. Emerging capabilities, such as the integration of real-time data and the use of digital twins, promise to enhance the precision and impact of generative design. These innovations will enable industries to further align product development with CE principles, driving progress toward a more sustainable and resource-efficient future.

Enhancing Product Longevity Through Predictive Maintenance with AI

Predictive maintenance powered by AI is revolutionizing how industries manage and extend the lifespan of products. By leveraging ML algorithms, real-time data analysis, and IoT devices, AI-driven predictive maintenance identifies potential issues before they lead to failures, ensuring timely interventions. This proactive approach significantly enhances product longevity, reduces waste, and aligns with the principles of the CE by promoting resource efficiency and sustainability.

The Importance of Product Longevity

Extending product lifespan is a key strategy for reducing environmental impact and conserving resources. Longer-lasting products minimize the need for frequent replacements, reducing material consumption and waste generation. Predictive maintenance supports this goal by optimizing the use of resources and preventing premature disposal due to avoidable malfunctions or breakdowns.

Traditional maintenance methods, such as scheduled or reactive maintenance, are either inefficient or insufficient for achieving maximum product longevity. Scheduled maintenance can lead to unnecessary servicing or missed issues, while reactive maintenance often results in costly downtime and significant resource losses. Predictive maintenance, enabled by AI, overcomes these limitations by providing precise, real-time insights that allow for timely and efficient maintenance actions.

How Predictive Maintenance Works

Predictive maintenance uses AI to monitor product performance and predict when maintenance is required. This process involves several key components:

- **Data Collection:** Sensors and IoT devices embedded in products collect data on operational parameters such as temperature, vibration, pressure, and usage patterns. This data is transmitted to centralized systems for analysis.
- **Data Analysis:** ML algorithms process the collected data to identify patterns and anomalies that indicate potential issues. These algorithms learn from historical data to refine their predictions and improve accuracy over time.
- **Maintenance Predictions:** AI systems predict when and where maintenance will be needed, allowing users to address issues before they escalate. These predictions are often accompanied by recommendations for specific actions, such as part replacements or system recalibrations.
- **Automated Alerts:** Predictive maintenance systems generate automated alerts for operators or users, ensuring that necessary actions are taken promptly. This minimizes the risk of unexpected failures and extends the life of the product.

Applications Across Industries

AI-driven predictive maintenance is being implemented across various industries to enhance product longevity:

- **Manufacturing:** In manufacturing, predictive maintenance monitors machinery and equipment to prevent unplanned downtime. For example, AI systems detect wear and tear in production line components, allowing for timely repairs and replacements that extend the lifespan of equipment.
- **Automotive:** Automakers integrate predictive maintenance into vehicles to monitor engine performance, battery health, and tire conditions. This ensures that vehicles remain operational for longer periods and reduces the frequency of replacements.
- **Energy:** In the energy sector, predictive maintenance is used to monitor wind turbines, solar panels, and other infrastructure. AI systems detect anomalies such as declining efficiency or mechanical wear, enabling timely interventions and prolonged asset life.
- **Healthcare:** Medical device manufacturers use predictive maintenance to monitor equipment such as MRI machines and ventilators. This ensures consistent performance and reduces the risk of device failures, extending the usability of critical medical technologies.
- **Consumer Electronics:** Predictive maintenance in electronics monitors battery health, processor performance, and system stability. AI tools notify users when maintenance actions, such as software updates or battery replacements, are needed to extend device lifespans.

Benefits of Predictive Maintenance

The benefits of predictive maintenance include:

- **Resource Efficiency:** By addressing issues before they escalate, predictive maintenance reduces resource consumption associated with repairs and replacements. This aligns with CE principles by keeping products in use for longer and minimizing waste.
- **Cost Savings:** Proactive maintenance reduces the costs associated with reactive repairs, downtime, and unplanned

replacements. Businesses and consumers benefit from lower operating costs and fewer disruptions.

- **Reduced Environmental Impact:** Extending the lifespan of products reduces the demand for raw materials and energy used in manufacturing new items. This contributes to lower greenhouse gas emissions and less environmental degradation.
- **Improved Reliability:** Predictive maintenance enhances product reliability by ensuring that systems function optimally. This builds consumer trust and promotes sustainable consumption practices.

Challenges in Implementation

Despite its advantages, implementing predictive maintenance with AI faces challenges such as:

- **High Initial Costs:** The installation of sensors, IoT devices, and AI systems requires significant investment. These costs may be prohibitive for SMEs.
- **Data Integration:** Predictive maintenance relies on comprehensive data from various sources. Integrating these data streams into a unified system can be complex and resource-intensive.
- **Technical Expertise:** Developing and maintaining AI-driven predictive maintenance systems requires specialized skills. Many organizations face challenges in recruiting or training personnel with the necessary expertise.
- **Scalability:** Scaling predictive maintenance across large fleets of products or facilities requires robust infrastructure and coordination, which can be logistically challenging.

Future Directions

As AI technologies continue to evolve, predictive maintenance will become more accessible, accurate, and scalable. Innovations such as advanced ML models, real-time analytics, and digital twins will further enhance its capabilities. By addressing current challenges and embracing these advancements, industries can maximize product longevity, reduce waste, and contribute to a more sustainable and resource-efficient future.

Chapter 5: AI-Driven Business Models in the Circular Economy

The transition to a CE requires innovative business models that promote resource efficiency, waste reduction, and sustainable consumption. AI is a key enabler of these models, offering advanced tools to optimize operations, enhance customer engagement, and create value from circular practices. This chapter explores how AI drives the development and implementation of business models such as product-as-a-service, sharing platforms, and reverse logistics. By integrating AI technologies, businesses can unlock new opportunities for growth while aligning with CE principles and fostering a sustainable future.

AI-Powered Sharing and Leasing Platforms

AI is revolutionizing the sharing and leasing economy by enabling smarter, more efficient, and scalable platforms that align with the principles of the CE. Sharing and leasing platforms focus on maximizing the use of resources by facilitating shared access to goods and services, reducing the need for ownership, and promoting resource efficiency. AI-powered technologies enhance these platforms by optimizing operations, improving user experiences, and enabling data-driven decision-making.

The Role of AI in Sharing and Leasing Platforms

AI supports sharing and leasing platforms by automating key processes, personalizing services, and improving resource utilization. These platforms rely on AI to analyze user behavior, predict demand, optimize logistics, and ensure seamless interactions between users and service providers. By leveraging ML, predictive analytics, and IoT integration, AI-powered platforms create value for users while reducing environmental impact.

Optimizing Resource Utilization

One of the key benefits of AI in sharing and leasing platforms is its ability to optimize resource utilization. AI algorithms analyze data on resource availability, usage patterns, and demand fluctuations to ensure that resources are allocated efficiently. For example, in shared mobility services, AI predicts peak demand times and locations, ensuring that vehicles are available where they are needed most. Similarly, in equipment leasing, AI identifies underutilized assets and suggests ways to increase their usage.

This optimization reduces idle time for resources, maximizing their utility and minimizing waste. It also lowers operational costs for service providers, making sharing and leasing models more economically viable and environmentally sustainable.

Predicting Demand and Supply

AI-powered predictive analytics enable sharing and leasing platforms to anticipate user needs and adjust supply accordingly. By analyzing historical usage data, seasonal trends, and external factors such as weather or events, AI systems forecast demand with high accuracy. This allows service providers to prepare for fluctuations, such as increasing the availability of shared vehicles during peak commuting hours or adjusting inventory for leased equipment during seasonal demand spikes.

AI also predicts supply constraints, such as maintenance requirements or asset downtime, ensuring that disruptions are minimized and service quality is maintained. These capabilities enhance user satisfaction while supporting resource efficiency.

Personalizing User Experiences

AI enhances the user experience on sharing and leasing platforms by personalizing services based on individual preferences and behaviors. ML algorithms analyze user data to recommend tailored options, such as suggesting vehicles or equipment that meet specific needs or offering personalized pricing plans.

For instance, in peer-to-peer sharing platforms, AI matches users with assets or services that best suit their requirements, such as recommending shared office spaces based on location, amenities, and budget. This personalization fosters user loyalty and encourages greater participation in sharing and leasing models.

Enhancing Logistics and Operations

Logistics and operational efficiency are critical for the success of sharing and leasing platforms. AI-powered systems optimize logistics by analyzing real-time data on asset locations, user demand, and transportation networks. For example, AI can plan the most efficient routes for delivering leased equipment or repositioning shared vehicles to high-demand areas.

AI also streamlines operations by automating tasks such as booking management, payment processing, and customer support. Chatbots and virtual assistants, powered by natural language processing, handle user inquiries and provide real-time assistance, improving the overall platform experience.

Ensuring Maintenance and Reliability

AI plays a crucial role in maintaining the reliability of shared and leased assets. Predictive maintenance systems monitor the condition of assets in real time, using data from IoT sensors and ML algorithms to detect potential issues before they lead to failures. This ensures that assets remain operational and safe for users, reducing downtime and repair costs.

For example, in bike-sharing platforms, AI monitors factors such as tire pressure, battery levels (in electric bikes), and structural integrity, scheduling maintenance when needed. This proactive approach extends the lifespan of shared assets and minimizes disruptions for users.

Applications Across Industries

AI-powered sharing and leasing platforms are transforming various industries:

- **Transportation:** Ride-sharing and car-sharing platforms use AI to optimize vehicle allocation, predict demand, and provide real-time navigation assistance.
- **Real Estate:** Co-living and shared office spaces leverage AI to match users with spaces that meet their needs, enhancing occupancy rates and resource efficiency.
- **Equipment Rental:** AI streamlines equipment leasing processes by predicting demand, optimizing inventory management, and ensuring timely delivery.
- **Consumer Goods:** Platforms for sharing appliances, tools, and recreational equipment use AI to facilitate seamless transactions and enhance user satisfaction.

Challenges and Future Directions

Despite their benefits, AI-powered sharing and leasing platforms face challenges such as data privacy concerns, high implementation costs, and the need for robust digital infrastructure. Ensuring equitable access to these platforms and addressing potential biases in AI algorithms are also critical considerations.

As technology advances, AI's role in sharing and leasing platforms will continue to grow. Emerging innovations, such as blockchain integration for secure transactions and advanced IoT connectivity for real-time asset tracking, promise to further enhance platform efficiency and scalability. By overcoming current challenges, AI-powered sharing and leasing platforms can drive sustainable resource use, reduce waste, and support the transition to a CE.

Predictive Analytics for Subscription-Based Models

Predictive analytics, powered by AI, has become a cornerstone of subscription-based business models, enabling companies to optimize operations, enhance customer experiences, and align with CE principles. By analyzing data on user behavior, consumption patterns, and market trends, predictive analytics provides actionable insights that improve decision-making and resource efficiency. These capabilities are crucial for subscription-based models, where maintaining customer satisfaction and operational efficiency are key to success.

Understanding Subscription-Based Models

Subscription-based models offer customers recurring access to products or services for a periodic fee, promoting usage over ownership. This approach supports CE principles by encouraging resource sharing, reducing overproduction, and extending product lifespans through repair and reuse. Predictive analytics enhances these models by anticipating customer needs, optimizing inventory, and streamlining service delivery.

Demand Forecasting and Inventory Optimization

One of the primary applications of predictive analytics in subscription-based models is demand forecasting. ML algorithms analyze historical usage data, customer preferences, and external factors such as seasonality to predict future demand accurately. These forecasts help businesses align their supply with customer needs, ensuring that resources are allocated efficiently.

For example, in a clothing rental service, predictive analytics can forecast demand for specific clothing types, sizes, or styles during certain seasons or events. This enables the company to optimize inventory levels, reducing the risk of overstocking or understocking while minimizing waste. Similarly, in a subscription box service, predictive analytics ensures that curated items match customer preferences, increasing satisfaction and reducing returns.

Customer Retention and Churn Prediction

Subscription-based models rely heavily on retaining customers over the long term. Predictive analytics helps businesses identify patterns and behaviors that indicate customer satisfaction or dissatisfaction, enabling proactive measures to reduce churn.

Churn Prediction

By analyzing data such as engagement frequency, payment history, and service usage, predictive models identify customers at risk of canceling their subscriptions. Businesses can then implement targeted retention strategies, such as personalized offers, improved customer support, or loyalty programs, to re-engage these customers.

Customer Lifetime Value (CLV)

Predictive analytics estimates the lifetime value of each customer, enabling businesses to focus their efforts on high-value subscribers. This ensures that marketing and retention strategies are cost-effective and aligned with long-term goals.

Personalized Recommendations

AI-driven predictive models analyze customer behavior and preferences to offer tailored product or service recommendations. For instance, a streaming platform might suggest content based on viewing habits, while a meal kit subscription could recommend recipes based on dietary preferences. These personalized experiences enhance customer satisfaction and loyalty.

Resource Management and Maintenance

In subscription-based models involving physical products, such as equipment rental or car sharing, predictive analytics plays a critical role in resource management and maintenance. By analyzing data from IoT sensors, usage logs, and environmental factors, predictive models optimize asset performance and availability.

Predictive Maintenance

Predictive analytics monitors the condition of shared assets in real time, identifying potential issues before they lead to failures. For example, in a bike-sharing service, AI can track wear and tear on components such as tires or chains, scheduling maintenance to prevent breakdowns. This proactive approach extends the lifespan of assets and reduces repair costs.

Utilization Optimization

Predictive models analyze usage patterns to ensure that assets are allocated where they are needed most. For example, in a tool-sharing subscription, AI can predict peak demand times and locations, enabling businesses to redistribute resources efficiently.

Pricing and Revenue Optimization

Predictive analytics supports dynamic pricing strategies in subscription-based models, helping businesses maximize revenue while remaining competitive. By analyzing market trends, customer willingness to pay, and competitor pricing, AI-driven models recommend optimal pricing structures that balance affordability with profitability.

For example, a software-as-a-service (SaaS) platform might use predictive analytics to offer discounted pricing to customers who show price sensitivity or introduce premium tiers for those willing to pay for advanced features. These strategies ensure that pricing remains flexible and responsive to market conditions.

Applications Across Industries

Predictive analytics is transforming subscription-based models across various sectors:

- **Media and Entertainment:** Streaming platforms use predictive analytics to recommend content, optimize user experiences, and reduce churn.
- **Retail:** Subscription box services leverage predictive models to curate personalized product selections and anticipate inventory needs.
- **Transportation:** Car-sharing and ride-sharing services use predictive analytics to optimize fleet allocation and pricing.
- **Healthcare:** Predictive analytics in telemedicine subscriptions anticipates patient needs and ensures timely service delivery.
- **Food and Beverage:** Meal kit subscriptions utilize AI to predict ingredient demand and reduce food waste.

Challenges and Future Directions

While predictive analytics offers significant advantages for subscription-based models, challenges such as data privacy concerns, integration complexities, and high implementation costs must be addressed. Ensuring transparency and fairness in AI-driven recommendations is also critical to maintaining customer trust.

As AI technologies continue to advance, predictive analytics will become more sophisticated and accessible. Innovations such as real-time data integration, advanced ML models, and blockchain-enabled transparency will further enhance the effectiveness of predictive analytics in subscription-based models. By overcoming current challenges and embracing these advancements, businesses can create sustainable, customer-centric subscription services that support the goals of the CE.

Optimizing Reverse Logistics with AI

Reverse logistics is a critical component of the CE, focusing on the process of returning products, materials, or resources from consumers back to manufacturers for reuse, refurbishment, recycling, or proper disposal. AI is transforming reverse logistics by providing advanced tools to optimize operations, improve efficiency, and reduce waste. By leveraging predictive analytics, ML, and real-time data processing, AI enhances decision-making and streamlines the reverse flow of materials, aligning with CE principles and promoting sustainable resource management.

Understanding Reverse Logistics

Reverse logistics involves activities such as product returns, end-of-life product recovery, recycling, and material reintegration into supply chains. Unlike traditional forward logistics, which is linear and focused on delivering goods to consumers, reverse logistics is more complex, involving uncertain quantities, variable product conditions, and multi-stakeholder coordination. Inefficient reverse logistics can lead to increased costs, resource wastage, and environmental impact.

AI addresses these challenges by automating key processes, providing actionable insights, and enabling data-driven strategies to optimize reverse logistics systems.

Predictive Analytics for Return Management

AI-powered predictive analytics plays a crucial role in managing product returns, a significant aspect of reverse logistics. By analyzing historical data, customer behavior, and market trends, predictive models forecast return rates and patterns, allowing businesses to prepare and allocate resources effectively.

Forecasting Returns

Predictive analytics estimates the volume and timing of returns, helping organizations adjust logistics operations accordingly. For example, during holiday seasons or product launch periods, businesses can anticipate higher return rates and ensure sufficient resources for handling them.

Analyzing Return Reasons

AI analyzes patterns in return data to identify common reasons for returns, such as defective products, incorrect orders, or unmet expectations. These insights enable companies to address root causes and reduce return rates over time.

Optimizing Return Policies

AI helps businesses design return policies that balance customer satisfaction with operational efficiency. For instance, predictive models can identify which products or regions require stricter return guidelines to minimize logistical burdens.

Improving Sorting and Classification

One of the biggest challenges in reverse logistics is sorting and classifying returned products based on their condition and potential for reuse. AI-powered systems, particularly those using computer vision and ML, automate and enhance this process.

Automated Inspection

Computer vision systems equipped with AI analyze returned products to assess their condition, detect defects, and classify items as reusable, repairable, or recyclable. For example, AI can inspect electronics for physical damage or identify wearable parts in machinery for potential refurbishment.

Quality Grading

ML algorithms assign quality grades to returned items, enabling efficient sorting and decision-making. This ensures that high-quality items are prioritized for resale, while lower-quality ones are directed to recycling or disposal.

Reducing Errors

Automated sorting reduces human errors and speeds up processing times, improving the overall efficiency of reverse logistics operations.

Optimizing Transportation and Logistics

Transportation and logistics are central to reverse logistics, and AI enhances these processes through route optimization, fleet management, and real-time tracking.

Route Optimization

AI-driven systems analyze factors such as distance, traffic conditions, and fuel efficiency to optimize transportation routes for collecting and redistributing returned items. This minimizes transportation costs, reduces emissions, and improves operational efficiency.

Dynamic Allocation

Predictive analytics allocates returned items to the most appropriate destinations, such as repair centers, recycling facilities, or warehouses, based on real-time data and demand forecasts. This ensures efficient resource utilization and minimizes unnecessary transportation.

Real-Time Tracking

IoT-enabled devices integrated with AI provide real-time updates on the location and condition of returned items. This transparency enhances accountability and coordination across stakeholders in the reverse logistics process.

Facilitating Resource Recovery

AI supports resource recovery by identifying opportunities for reusing, refurbishing, or recycling materials from returned products.

Material Identification

AI-powered systems analyze product composition to identify valuable materials that can be recovered and reintegrated into production cycles. For instance, AI can detect rare metals in electronic waste or reusable fabrics in returned garments.

Recycling Optimization

ML algorithms optimize recycling processes by analyzing material properties and recommending the most efficient recycling methods. This reduces waste and ensures higher recovery rates.

Enabling Closed-Loop Systems

AI facilitates closed-loop manufacturing by ensuring that recovered materials meet quality standards for reintegration into production. This supports CE goals by keeping resources in circulation and reducing reliance on virgin materials.

Enhancing Customer Experience

Reverse logistics often involves customer-facing processes, and AI enhances these interactions to improve satisfaction and streamline operations.

Streamlined Returns

AI-powered chatbots and self-service platforms guide customers through the return process, ensuring clarity and convenience. These systems provide real-time updates on return statuses and expected resolutions.

Personalized Solutions

Predictive analytics offers personalized recommendations for customers, such as repair options or trade-in programs, based on their purchase history and preferences. This encourages sustainable behaviors and builds customer loyalty.

Reducing Friction

By automating and optimizing reverse logistics processes, AI reduces delays and errors that can frustrate customers, ensuring a smoother experience.

Challenges and Future Directions

Despite its advantages, implementing AI in reverse logistics faces challenges such as high initial costs, data integration issues, and the need for skilled personnel. Ensuring data privacy and security is also critical, given the sensitive nature of customer and product data involved in reverse logistics.

Looking ahead, advancements in AI technologies, such as blockchain integration for supply chain transparency and advanced robotics for automated sorting, promise to further enhance reverse logistics systems. By addressing these challenges and leveraging AI's potential, businesses can create efficient, sustainable reverse logistics operations that align with CE principles and contribute to a more resource-efficient future.

Challenges in Scaling AI-Driven Business Models

Scaling AI-driven business models presents significant opportunities for efficiency, innovation, and sustainability. However, it also introduces a range of challenges that businesses must address to fully realize the potential of AI. These challenges span technological, organizational, ethical, and regulatory domains, requiring comprehensive strategies to overcome barriers and achieve successful implementation at scale.

Data Availability and Quality

1. Data Fragmentation:

AI systems rely on large volumes of high-quality data to generate accurate insights. In many organizations, data is fragmented across silos or stored in inconsistent formats, making it difficult to aggregate and analyze. This fragmentation limits the effectiveness of AI models and impedes scalability.

2. Data Quality Issues:

Poor data quality, including inaccuracies, inconsistencies, and incomplete datasets, undermines the reliability of AI-driven predictions and recommendations. Ensuring clean, structured, and comprehensive data is essential for scaling AI-driven business models.

3. Data Access and Integration:

Integrating data from diverse sources, such as internal systems, third-party platforms, and IoT devices, is a complex task. Businesses must invest in robust data infrastructure and integration capabilities to enable seamless access and usage.

High Implementation Costs

1. Upfront Investments:

Scaling AI-driven models requires significant upfront investment in hardware, software, and skilled personnel. Advanced AI tools, cloud computing infrastructure, and specialized talent often come with high costs that can be prohibitive, particularly for SMEs.

2. Operational Costs:

Ongoing operational costs, such as data storage, model training, and system maintenance, increase as AI systems scale. Balancing these costs with expected returns on investment (ROI) is a critical challenge for businesses.

3. Technology Upgrades:

Scaling AI-driven business models often necessitates upgrading existing technology infrastructure to support the computational demands of AI. These upgrades can be costly and time-consuming.

Workforce and Organizational Challenges

1. Skill Gaps:

Implementing and scaling AI-driven business models require a workforce with expertise in data science, ML, and AI development. Many organizations struggle to find or train personnel with the necessary skills, creating a significant bottleneck in scaling efforts.

2. Resistance to Change:

Organizational resistance to adopting AI-driven approaches can hinder scalability. Employees and stakeholders accustomed to traditional business models may be reluctant to embrace AI, fearing job displacement or disruption to established processes.

3. Collaboration and Alignment:

Scaling AI requires collaboration across departments and alignment of objectives. Silos within organizations can create barriers to effective implementation and limit the scalability of AI initiatives.

Technological Complexity

1. Model Scalability:

AI models developed for small-scale use may not perform effectively when applied to larger datasets or more complex systems. Ensuring that AI models are scalable and robust is a significant technical challenge.

2. Real-Time Processing:

Scaling AI-driven business models often involves processing large volumes of data in real time. Achieving this requires advanced computational capabilities and efficient algorithms, which can be difficult to implement at scale.

3. System Integration:

Integrating AI systems with existing workflows, software, and hardware can be technically complex. Legacy systems may lack the compatibility needed to support AI-driven solutions, requiring significant modifications or replacements.

Ethical and Regulatory Concerns

1. Data Privacy and Security:

As AI systems scale, they process increasingly large amounts of sensitive data. Ensuring data privacy and protecting against breaches are critical challenges, especially in industries with strict regulatory requirements.

2. Bias and Fairness:

Scaling AI-driven models can amplify biases present in training data, leading to unfair outcomes. Addressing bias and ensuring fairness in AI systems require rigorous testing and continuous monitoring.

3. Regulatory Compliance:

Businesses must navigate complex and evolving regulatory frameworks related to AI, data usage, and consumer rights. Compliance challenges become more pronounced as AI systems scale across regions with varying regulations.

Scalability Across Diverse Markets

1. Localization Challenges:

Scaling AI-driven business models to global markets requires localization to account for differences in languages, cultures, and regulations. Adapting AI systems to meet the specific needs of diverse markets is resource-intensive.

2. Infrastructure Disparities:

Regions with limited digital infrastructure may lack the connectivity and computational power needed to support AI-driven solutions. These disparities pose challenges for scaling AI to underserved markets.

3. Consumer Acceptance:

Scaling AI-driven business models requires building trust and acceptance among consumers. Addressing concerns related to AI transparency, ethics, and reliability is critical for driving adoption at scale.

Future Directions

To overcome these challenges, businesses must invest in robust data infrastructure, foster a culture of innovation, and prioritize ethical AI practices. Collaboration with technology providers, regulators, and industry stakeholders is essential for addressing scalability issues and ensuring that AI-driven business models deliver sustainable value. By addressing these barriers, organizations can unlock the full potential of AI to transform industries and support the goals of the CE.

Chapter 6: AI and Circular Supply Chains

Circular supply chains represent a transformative shift from traditional linear models, emphasizing resource efficiency, waste reduction, and material recirculation. AI plays a pivotal role in enabling this transition by optimizing processes, enhancing transparency, and facilitating closed-loop systems. This chapter explores how AI-powered tools, such as predictive analytics, IoT integration, and ML, are revolutionizing supply chain management. By improving resource tracking, logistics, and material recovery, AI supports the creation of circular supply chains that align with the principles of the CE and contribute to sustainable business practices.

AI for End-to-End Supply Chain Transparency

Supply chain transparency is a cornerstone of sustainable business practices and the CE, enabling organizations to monitor and manage resources effectively from raw material sourcing to end-of-life recovery. AI is transforming end-to-end supply chain transparency by leveraging advanced data analytics, IoT integration, and ML to provide real-time visibility, optimize operations, and ensure accountability across complex networks. These capabilities empower businesses to identify inefficiencies, reduce waste, and align supply chain activities with CE principles.

The Importance of Supply Chain Transparency

Supply chain transparency involves the ability to track and trace materials, products, and processes throughout the entire supply chain. Transparency ensures that stakeholders have access to accurate and timely information about resource flows, production methods, and environmental impacts. This visibility is critical for addressing challenges such as resource mismanagement, waste generation, and non-compliance with environmental and ethical standards.

Traditional supply chain management systems often rely on fragmented data and manual processes, which limit their ability to provide comprehensive transparency. AI overcomes these limitations by automating data collection and analysis, enabling businesses to gain real-time insights into their supply chains and make data-driven decisions.

Real-Time Data Collection and Integration

AI enhances supply chain transparency by integrating data from diverse sources, such as IoT devices, sensors, and enterprise systems. These technologies enable real-time tracking of materials and products as they move through the supply chain:

- **IoT Integration:** IoT devices embedded in products and infrastructure collect data on parameters such as location, condition, and usage. AI processes this data to provide a clear picture of resource flows and identify potential bottlenecks or inefficiencies.
- **Sensor Technology:** Sensors monitor critical metrics such as temperature, humidity, and pressure, ensuring that products are stored and transported under optimal conditions. AI analyzes sensor data to detect anomalies and prevent quality degradation or waste.
- **Data Standardization:** AI-driven tools standardize and consolidate data from multiple sources, ensuring consistency and accuracy. This integration eliminates silos and creates a unified view of the supply chain.

Predictive Analytics for Visibility

Predictive analytics powered by AI enhances supply chain transparency by forecasting potential disruptions and optimizing resource allocation:

- **Demand Forecasting:** AI analyzes historical sales data, market trends, and external factors to predict demand fluctuations. This ensures that supply chains are aligned with actual needs, reducing overproduction and resource waste.

- **Risk Identification:** Predictive models identify risks such as supply chain disruptions, equipment failures, or environmental hazards. By anticipating these issues, businesses can take proactive measures to mitigate their impact.
- **Inventory Optimization:** AI optimizes inventory levels by predicting stock requirements and ensuring that resources are available where and when they are needed. This reduces excess inventory and minimizes waste.

Enhanced Traceability with Blockchain and AI

Blockchain technology, when integrated with AI, significantly enhances traceability in supply chains. Blockchain creates a secure and immutable ledger of transactions, while AI analyzes this data to provide actionable insights:

- **Material Provenance:** AI traces the origin of raw materials to ensure compliance with environmental and ethical standards. For example, businesses can verify whether materials are sustainably sourced or free from conflict zones.
- **Lifecycle Tracking:** AI tracks the lifecycle of products from production to disposal, providing transparency into their environmental impact. This information supports circular practices such as recycling, refurbishment, and material recovery.
- **Fraud Prevention:** AI detects inconsistencies or irregularities in blockchain records, preventing fraud and ensuring the authenticity of supply chain data.

Applications Across Industries

AI-driven supply chain transparency is transforming various industries by enhancing visibility and accountability:

- **Manufacturing:** AI tracks raw materials and components throughout production, ensuring efficient resource use and reducing waste.
- **Retail:** Retailers use AI to monitor product movements, optimize inventory, and provide consumers with transparency into product origins and sustainability certifications.
- **Food and Agriculture:** AI ensures traceability of food products, from farm to fork, improving food safety and reducing waste in agricultural supply chains.
- **Pharmaceuticals:** AI monitors the storage and transportation of medicines, ensuring compliance with temperature and handling requirements to maintain product integrity.

Challenges in Implementing AI for Transparency

Despite its benefits, implementing AI for end-to-end supply chain transparency presents challenges:

- **Data Privacy:** Collecting and sharing supply chain data involves sensitive information that must be protected to comply with privacy regulations and maintain stakeholder trust.
- **High Costs:** Implementing AI systems requires significant investment in technology, infrastructure, and skilled personnel. SMEs may face financial barriers.
- **Integration Complexity:** Integrating AI with existing supply chain systems can be technically complex and resource-intensive, particularly for organizations with legacy systems.
- **Data Quality Issues:** AI relies on accurate and comprehensive data. Incomplete or low-quality data can compromise the effectiveness of AI-driven insights.

Future Opportunities

As AI technologies continue to advance, their potential to enhance supply chain transparency will grow. Innovations such as real-time digital twins, advanced ML models, and AI-enabled sustainability dashboards promise to further improve visibility and accountability. By addressing current challenges and leveraging AI's capabilities, businesses can create supply chains that are transparent, efficient, and fully aligned with the principles of the CE.

AI in Circular Procurement Processes

Circular procurement is a vital component of the CE, focusing on purchasing practices that prioritize sustainability, resource efficiency, and waste minimization. By integrating AI into circular procurement processes, organizations can enhance decision-making, optimize resource use, and ensure compliance with sustainability goals. AI-driven tools enable businesses to analyze procurement data, identify opportunities for circular practices, and streamline supply chain operations. These advancements play a crucial role in transitioning to more sustainable procurement systems.

Understanding Circular Procurement

Circular procurement involves selecting goods and services that align with CE principles, emphasizing durability, repairability, recyclability, and the use of sustainable materials. Unlike traditional procurement, which often focuses solely on cost and functionality, circular procurement considers the entire lifecycle of products and their environmental impact. AI supports this shift by providing data-driven insights and automating key aspects of the procurement process.

Optimizing Supplier Selection

One of the primary applications of AI in circular procurement is optimizing supplier selection. By analyzing supplier data and market trends, AI-driven systems identify vendors that align with an organization's sustainability objectives:

- **Sustainability Assessment:** AI evaluates suppliers based on their sustainability practices, such as the use of recycled materials, adherence to ethical labor standards, and carbon reduction initiatives. This ensures that procurement decisions support environmental and social responsibility.
- **Performance Tracking:** ML algorithms monitor supplier performance over time, analyzing metrics such as on-time delivery, product quality, and environmental impact. These insights enable organizations to establish long-term partnerships with suppliers that consistently meet circular procurement criteria.
- **Risk Mitigation:** Predictive analytics identifies potential risks in the supply chain, such as non-compliance with environmental regulations or resource shortages. By anticipating these issues, businesses can proactively address them and maintain alignment with circular principles.

Enhancing Material Selection

AI plays a crucial role in material selection by analyzing data on material properties, availability, and environmental impact. This ensures that procurement decisions prioritize sustainable materials that support CE objectives:

- **Lifecycle Analysis:** AI integrates lifecycle data into procurement processes, evaluating the environmental impact of materials from extraction to disposal. This helps organizations select materials with lower carbon footprints and higher recyclability.
- **Promoting Recycled Content:** AI identifies opportunities to incorporate recycled materials into procurement decisions, reducing reliance on virgin resources. For example, procurement teams can use AI tools to prioritize suppliers that offer products made from post-consumer or post-industrial waste.
- **Material Substitution:** ML algorithms recommend sustainable alternatives to resource-intensive materials, such as biodegradable plastics or renewable fibers. This ensures

that products align with CE goals without compromising performance.

Streamlining Procurement Operations

AI-driven automation enhances the efficiency of circular procurement processes by streamlining operations and reducing manual workloads:

- **Automated Vendor Matching:** AI systems automatically match procurement needs with suitable vendors, saving time and ensuring alignment with circular criteria. These systems consider factors such as cost, availability, and sustainability certifications.
- **Smart Contracting:** AI supports the creation of smart contracts that include sustainability clauses, ensuring compliance with circular procurement standards. These contracts automate enforcement and reduce administrative burdens.
- **Spend Analysis:** Predictive analytics identifies patterns in procurement spending, highlighting opportunities to reduce costs and prioritize sustainable products. For example, AI can analyze bulk purchasing options to minimize packaging waste and transportation emissions.

Improving Transparency and Accountability

Transparency is critical for circular procurement, and AI enhances visibility into supply chains and procurement practices:

- **Traceability:** AI tracks the origins and lifecycle of procured products, ensuring compliance with sustainability standards. For instance, AI tools can verify the authenticity of recycled materials or certify that wood products come from sustainably managed forests.
- **Compliance Monitoring:** AI monitors compliance with environmental regulations and corporate sustainability goals,

providing real-time alerts for potential violations. This reduces the risk of non-compliance and enhances accountability.

- **Performance Reporting:** AI generates detailed reports on procurement performance, including metrics such as carbon emissions, resource use, and waste reduction. These reports help organizations demonstrate progress toward CE objectives and communicate achievements to stakeholders.

Applications Across Industries

AI-powered circular procurement is transforming practices across various sectors:

- **Construction:** AI prioritizes sustainable materials such as recycled concrete or reclaimed wood in construction projects, reducing resource extraction and waste.
- **Manufacturing:** Procurement teams use AI to source components made from recycled metals or biodegradable materials, ensuring product sustainability.
- **Retail:** Retailers leverage AI to identify suppliers that offer packaging made from recycled or reusable materials, supporting waste reduction initiatives.
- **Healthcare:** AI optimizes the procurement of medical supplies by prioritizing products with sustainable packaging and reduced environmental impact.

Challenges in AI-Driven Circular Procurement

Despite its potential, implementing AI in circular procurement faces challenges:

- **Data Availability:** Comprehensive data on supplier practices, material properties, and lifecycle impacts is essential for effective AI deployment. Limited access to such data can hinder decision-making.

- **Integration Costs:** Implementing AI-driven procurement systems requires significant investment in technology and training, which may pose barriers for smaller organizations.
- **Resistance to Change:** Adopting circular procurement practices often involves a cultural shift within organizations. Resistance to change can slow down implementation and limit effectiveness.
- **Ethical Considerations:** Ensuring that AI-driven decisions align with ethical values, such as fair labor practices and equitable resource distribution, is critical for building trust and accountability.

Future Opportunities

As AI technologies evolve, their applications in circular procurement will expand. Innovations such as blockchain-enabled traceability, advanced predictive analytics, and real-time supplier performance monitoring promise to further enhance the efficiency and sustainability of procurement processes. By addressing current challenges and leveraging AI capabilities, organizations can transform procurement into a powerful driver of the CE.

Optimizing Resource Loops with AI-Enabled Supply Chains

Resource loops are at the heart of the CE, focusing on keeping materials in use for as long as possible through reuse, refurbishment, recycling, and remanufacturing. AI is transforming the ability of supply chains to optimize resource loops by enabling real-time tracking, predictive analytics, and advanced decision-making. By integrating AI into supply chain operations, businesses can reduce waste, improve efficiency, and ensure the continual circulation of materials, aligning with CE principles.

The Role of AI in Resource Loop Optimization

AI enhances resource loops by providing visibility, automation, and intelligence across supply chain processes. From tracking material flows to enabling the reintegration of recovered resources, AI facilitates the seamless operation of closed-loop systems. These capabilities help businesses minimize resource extraction, reduce waste generation, and increase the use of secondary materials.

Real-Time Tracking and Visibility

Visibility is a foundational element for optimizing resource loops, and AI-driven tools provide unparalleled capabilities for tracking materials and products throughout their lifecycle:

- **IoT Integration:** IoT devices embedded in products or packaging capture data on location, condition, and usage. AI processes this data in real time, enabling businesses to monitor material flows and identify opportunities for reuse or recycling.
- **Digital Twins:** AI-enabled digital twins create virtual replicas of physical assets, allowing supply chain managers to simulate material flows and identify inefficiencies. These insights enable proactive decision-making to optimize resource utilization.
- **Traceability:** AI tracks the origin and lifecycle of materials, ensuring that recovered resources meet quality standards for reintegration. This transparency is critical for building trust in secondary material markets and supporting CE goals.

Predictive Analytics for Resource Recovery

AI-driven predictive analytics empowers businesses to anticipate resource recovery opportunities and optimize their use:

- **Demand Forecasting for Secondary Materials:** Predictive models analyze market trends and historical data to forecast demand for recycled or refurbished materials. This ensures that recovered resources are reintegrated into production cycles efficiently and at scale.

- **Proactive Maintenance:** AI predicts the need for maintenance or refurbishment of products, extending their lifespan and maximizing their utility. For example, in industries such as electronics or automotive, AI can identify when components need repair or replacement, reducing the need for new materials.
- **End-of-Life Predictions:** AI systems forecast the end-of-life phase of products, enabling businesses to plan for their recovery and reintegration. By anticipating disposal trends, companies can design effective reverse logistics systems to capture valuable resources.

Optimizing Reverse Logistics for Closed Loops

Reverse logistics is essential for closing resource loops, and AI significantly enhances its efficiency:

- **Route Optimization:** AI-driven logistics tools analyze transportation data to determine the most efficient routes for collecting end-of-life products or materials. This reduces fuel consumption, costs, and carbon emissions.
- **Dynamic Allocation:** Predictive analytics allocates recovered materials to the most appropriate destinations, such as refurbishment centers, recycling facilities, or remanufacturing plants. This ensures that resources are processed in a way that maximizes their value.
- **Automation in Sorting:** AI-powered computer vision systems automate the sorting of returned products, categorizing them by condition, material, or reuse potential. This speeds up processing times and reduces the labor required for manual sorting.

Facilitating Closed-Loop Manufacturing

AI supports closed-loop manufacturing systems by enabling the efficient reintegration of recovered resources into production cycles:

- **Quality Assurance:** AI systems analyze the quality of recovered materials to ensure they meet manufacturing standards. This reduces the risk of contamination or defects in final products, improving customer satisfaction and trust.
- **Material Matching:** ML algorithms match recovered materials with production needs, optimizing their use and reducing dependence on virgin resources. For instance, AI can determine the most suitable applications for recycled plastics or metals based on their properties.
- **Inventory Management:** AI manages inventories of secondary materials, ensuring that they are available when needed. This prevents resource shortages and minimizes storage costs, making closed-loop systems more economically viable.

Applications Across Industries

AI-enabled resource loops are transforming industries by enhancing sustainability and operational efficiency:

- **Automotive:** AI optimizes the recovery and reuse of materials such as steel, aluminum, and plastics from end-of-life vehicles. Components like engines and batteries are refurbished for reintegration into new products.
- **Electronics:** AI-driven systems facilitate the recovery of rare earth metals, circuit boards, and other valuable components from electronic waste, reducing reliance on virgin materials.
- **Textiles:** AI analyzes post-consumer textile waste to sort materials for recycling or reuse, enabling the production of new garments from recovered fibers.
- **Construction:** AI supports the recovery of materials such as concrete, wood, and steel from demolition waste, promoting their reuse in new building projects.

Challenges in Implementing AI for Resource Loops

Despite its potential, implementing AI for resource loop optimization presents challenges:

- **Data Integration:** Effective resource loops require data from multiple sources, including suppliers, manufacturers, and recyclers. Integrating these data streams into a cohesive system is a complex task.
- **High Costs:** Deploying AI systems for resource loop optimization requires significant investment in technology, training, and infrastructure. This can be a barrier for SMEs.
- **Regulatory Complexity:** Navigating varying regulations related to waste management, recycling, and material recovery across regions can complicate the implementation of AI-enabled resource loops.
- **Stakeholder Collaboration:** Closing resource loops requires collaboration among diverse stakeholders, including governments, businesses, and consumers. Aligning interests and ensuring data sharing can be challenging.

Future Opportunities

As AI technologies continue to advance, their potential to optimize resource loops will expand. Innovations such as blockchain-integrated traceability, advanced robotics for material recovery, and real-time analytics for resource forecasting promise to further enhance the efficiency and scalability of AI-enabled supply chains. By addressing current challenges and leveraging AI capabilities, businesses can create sustainable systems that minimize waste, maximize resource utility, and support the transition to a CE.

Overcoming Barriers to Circular Supply Chain Adoption

Circular supply chains, essential for advancing the principles of the CE, focus on resource efficiency, waste minimization, and material recirculation. However, adopting circular supply chains comes with significant barriers, including technological, financial, organizational, and regulatory challenges. Overcoming these obstacles requires strategic planning, collaboration, and leveraging advanced tools such as AI and data-driven decision-making to create sustainable, scalable systems.

Technological Challenges

1. Data Integration and Visibility:

One of the primary barriers to circular supply chain adoption is the lack of data integration and visibility across supply chain networks. Traditional supply chains often operate in silos, making it difficult to track resources and products throughout their lifecycle. Overcoming this challenge requires the implementation of technologies such as IoT devices and AI-driven platforms that provide real-time data on material flows, product conditions, and end-of-life stages.

2. Infrastructure Limitations:

Many regions lack the necessary infrastructure for circular supply chain operations, such as advanced recycling facilities or reverse logistics networks. Investments in technology and infrastructure, such as automated sorting systems and digital twins, are essential for enabling circular processes.

3. Technical Complexity of Material Recovery:

Recovering and reintegrating materials into production cycles can be technically complex, particularly for products composed of mixed materials or hazardous substances. AI-powered material identification and separation technologies can help streamline these processes, reducing inefficiencies and costs.

Financial Barriers

1. High Initial Investments:

Transitioning to circular supply chains often requires significant upfront investments in technology, infrastructure, and workforce training. These costs can be prohibitive, especially for SMEs. Addressing this barrier involves securing funding through government grants, public-private partnerships, or green financing initiatives.

2. Uncertain Return on Investment (ROI):

Circular supply chains may take time to deliver measurable financial benefits, such as cost savings from reduced resource use or revenue from secondary materials. Businesses must adopt long-term perspectives and implement performance metrics to evaluate the ROI of circular practices.

3. Economic Feasibility of Secondary Materials:

The cost of processing and reintegrating secondary materials often exceeds the cost of using virgin resources. To overcome this, businesses can adopt AI-driven tools to optimize material recovery processes, improve quality standards, and reduce operational costs, making secondary materials more economically viable.

Organizational Challenges

1. Resistance to Change:

Implementing circular supply chains requires fundamental changes to traditional business models and supply chain practices. Resistance from stakeholders, including employees, suppliers, and customers, can hinder progress. Overcoming this barrier involves fostering a culture of innovation and providing education and training on the benefits of circular supply chains.

2. Skill Gaps:

Circular supply chains rely on advanced technologies and specialized knowledge, such as data analytics, reverse logistics, and material science. Addressing skill gaps requires investments in workforce development, including training programs and partnerships with academic institutions.

3. Coordination Across Stakeholders:

Circular supply chains involve collaboration among diverse stakeholders, including suppliers, manufacturers, recyclers, and policymakers. Misalignment of goals or priorities can create barriers to implementation. Establishing clear communication channels and aligning incentives across stakeholders are critical for overcoming these challenges.

Regulatory and Policy Challenges

1. Inconsistent Regulations:

Regulatory frameworks for waste management, recycling, and resource recovery vary significantly across regions, creating complexity for businesses operating in global supply chains. Standardizing regulations and harmonizing policies can help reduce these inconsistencies and facilitate circular supply chain adoption.

2. Lack of Incentives:

In many regions, there are insufficient incentives to adopt circular practices, such as tax benefits, subsidies, or penalties for non-compliance with sustainability goals. Advocating for supportive policies and collaborating with governments to establish financial incentives can accelerate the transition to circular supply chains.

3. Compliance Costs:

Ensuring compliance with environmental and CE regulations can increase operational costs. Businesses can leverage AI-driven compliance monitoring tools to streamline reporting and reduce the burden of regulatory adherence.

Cultural and Market Barriers

1. Consumer Awareness and Demand:

Limited consumer awareness of the environmental benefits of circular supply chains can hinder demand for sustainable products. Businesses must invest in marketing and education campaigns to build consumer awareness and drive demand for circular products.

2. Competition with Linear Models:

Linear supply chains are often more cost-efficient and well-established, creating competition for circular systems. Demonstrating the long-term value of circular supply chains, including environmental benefits and brand reputation, is critical for overcoming this barrier.

3. Market Fragmentation:

Fragmented markets for secondary materials can limit their availability and quality. Collaborating with industry associations and policymakers to establish standardized markets and quality certifications for secondary materials can address this challenge.

Solutions and Opportunities

1. Collaboration Across Industries:

Cross-industry collaboration is essential for sharing best practices, pooling resources, and developing scalable solutions for circular supply chains. Platforms for knowledge exchange and partnerships can accelerate progress.

2. **Leveraging Technology:**

Technologies such as AI, IoT, and blockchain are critical for overcoming many barriers to circular supply chain adoption. These tools enhance transparency, optimize operations, and enable data-driven decision-making.

3. **Incentivizing Innovation:**

Governments and industry leaders can encourage innovation by providing funding and recognition for businesses that develop and implement circular supply chain solutions. This creates a competitive advantage for early adopters and accelerates the transition to a CE.

By addressing these barriers and implementing targeted strategies, businesses can overcome challenges in adopting circular supply chains and create systems that are resilient, sustainable, and aligned with CE principles.

Chapter 7: Ethical and Governance Considerations

The integration of AI into CE practices presents significant opportunities for sustainability, but it also raises critical ethical and governance considerations. From ensuring transparency and fairness in decision-making to addressing data privacy and accountability, businesses and policymakers must navigate complex challenges to align AI-driven solutions with societal values. This chapter explores the ethical dilemmas and governance frameworks needed to guide the responsible adoption of AI in CE systems. By addressing these considerations, organizations can build trust, ensure equitable outcomes, and foster long-term sustainability.

Ethical Use of AI in the Circular Economy

The CE relies on innovative technologies, including AI, to drive resource efficiency, reduce waste, and promote sustainability. However, the integration of AI into CE systems raises critical ethical concerns that must be addressed to ensure responsible and equitable implementation. These concerns include data privacy, transparency, accountability, and fairness. By embedding ethical principles into AI-driven CE practices, organizations can align technological advancements with societal values and foster trust among stakeholders.

Ensuring Data Privacy and Security

1. Data Collection Concerns:

AI systems in the CE often rely on large volumes of data collected from sensors, IoT devices, and user interactions. This data includes sensitive information, such as consumer behavior, supply chain activities, and material flows. Protecting the privacy of individuals and organizations involved in these processes is a critical ethical challenge.

2. Risk of Data Misuse:

Improper handling of data can lead to misuse, such as unauthorized sharing, surveillance, or exploitation. Businesses must implement robust data governance policies to ensure that data is collected, stored, and used ethically, adhering to legal and regulatory requirements.

3. Securing Systems Against Breaches:

AI systems are vulnerable to cybersecurity threats, including hacking and data breaches. These risks can compromise the integrity of CE systems and erode stakeholder trust. Advanced encryption, regular security audits, and compliance with data protection standards are essential for mitigating these risks.

Promoting Transparency and Explainability

1. Opaque Decision-Making:

Many AI models, especially those based on deep learning, operate as "black boxes," making it difficult for stakeholders to understand how decisions are made. This lack of transparency can lead to mistrust and skepticism, particularly when AI systems are used to allocate resources or determine the recyclability of materials.

2. Explainable AI (XAI):

To address this challenge, organizations should adopt explainable AI (XAI) frameworks that provide clear and interpretable insights into decision-making processes. XAI ensures that stakeholders understand the rationale behind AI-driven decisions, fostering trust and accountability.

3. Stakeholder Involvement:

Transparent communication with stakeholders, including consumers, suppliers, and regulators, is critical for ethical AI use in the CE. Organizations should actively engage stakeholders in discussions about how AI systems are designed, implemented, and governed.

Ensuring Fairness and Equity

1. Avoiding Algorithmic Bias:

AI systems can inadvertently perpetuate or amplify biases present in training data, leading to unfair outcomes. For example, biased algorithms might prioritize certain materials or regions over others, creating inequities in resource allocation or access to recycling programs.

2. Inclusive Data Practices:

Ethical AI development requires diverse and representative datasets that reflect the needs and perspectives of all stakeholders. By addressing data biases during the design phase, organizations can create AI systems that promote fairness and equity.

3. Equal Access to Benefits:

CE systems powered by AI must ensure that benefits, such as cost savings, resource efficiency, and waste reduction, are distributed equitably across communities. Organizations should prioritize initiatives that address the needs of underserved or marginalized groups, avoiding the concentration of benefits among privileged stakeholders.

Accountability and Governance

1. Clear Accountability Mechanisms:

The use of AI in the CE requires clear accountability mechanisms to address potential failures, such as incorrect predictions or unethical outcomes. Organizations must define roles and responsibilities for AI governance, ensuring that accountability is shared among developers, operators, and decision-makers.

2. Ethical AI Frameworks:

Adopting ethical AI frameworks and guidelines, such as those developed by global organizations, can help businesses align their AI practices with ethical standards. These frameworks provide principles for fairness, transparency, accountability, and privacy.

3. Regulatory Compliance:

Businesses must navigate complex and evolving regulatory landscapes related to AI and sustainability. Ensuring compliance with relevant laws, such as data protection regulations and environmental standards, is essential for ethical AI use.

Balancing Efficiency with Human Oversight

1. Avoiding Over-Reliance on AI:

While AI can optimize CE systems, over-reliance on automated processes may lead to ethical blind spots. For example, fully automated sorting systems might overlook valuable materials that require manual intervention for recovery.

2. Human Oversight:

Incorporating human oversight into AI-driven systems ensures that ethical considerations are addressed in decision-making processes. Human operators can provide contextual insights and judgment that complement AI capabilities, preventing unintended consequences.

3. Ethical Trade-Offs:

Organizations must navigate trade-offs between efficiency and ethics. For instance, maximizing resource recovery may conflict with privacy concerns when tracking individual consumer behavior. Balancing these competing priorities requires careful deliberation and stakeholder engagement.

Fostering Public Trust

1. Building Transparency in Operations:

Ethical AI use in the CE relies on earning and maintaining public trust. Organizations should openly communicate their efforts to address ethical challenges, demonstrating their commitment to responsible AI practices.

2. Educational Initiatives:

Public awareness campaigns and educational initiatives can help demystify AI technologies and highlight their benefits in promoting sustainability. These efforts empower consumers to make informed choices and participate actively in CE systems.

3. Corporate Responsibility:

Companies must position ethical AI use as a core component of their corporate social responsibility (CSR) strategies. By embedding ethical principles into their operations, businesses can enhance their reputation and contribute to broader sustainability goals.

Future Directions

Ethical AI use in the CE requires ongoing dialogue, innovation, and collaboration among stakeholders. By addressing challenges related to data privacy, transparency, fairness, and accountability, organizations can create AI-driven systems that align with societal values and support the transition to sustainable resource management.

Privacy and Data Security Challenges

As AI becomes increasingly integral to the CE, the collection, storage, and analysis of large volumes of data raise significant privacy and data security challenges. These challenges affect individuals, organizations, and supply chains, requiring robust safeguards to ensure that sensitive information is protected. Addressing these issues is critical for fostering trust, ensuring compliance with regulations, and aligning AI-driven CE systems with ethical standards.

Data Collection Concerns

1. Volume of Data:

AI systems in CE rely on vast amounts of data from sources such as IoT devices, sensors, supply chains, and user interactions. The scale of this data collection increases the risk of exposing sensitive information, making privacy a top concern for stakeholders.

2. Personal Data Risks:

In systems that involve consumer interactions, such as sharing platforms or subscription services, personal data such as names, addresses, and usage patterns are often collected. Mismanagement or unauthorized access to this data can lead to privacy violations and erode user trust.

3. Proprietary Information:

Circular supply chains often require data sharing between organizations, including suppliers, manufacturers, and recyclers. This can involve proprietary information, such as production methods or material compositions, which must be protected to avoid competitive disadvantages.

Data Storage Vulnerabilities

1. Centralized Storage Risks:

Many organizations store collected data in centralized databases, which become high-value targets for cyberattacks. If these databases are breached, sensitive information can be exposed or stolen, leading to financial and reputational damage.

2. Cloud Storage Concerns:

Cloud-based storage solutions offer scalability but also introduce vulnerabilities related to third-party access and shared infrastructure. Ensuring data security in cloud environments requires robust encryption and stringent access controls.

3. Retention Policies:

Storing data for extended periods increases the likelihood of unauthorized access or misuse. Defining clear data retention policies and regularly deleting unnecessary data are essential for minimizing storage risks.

Cybersecurity Threats

1. Hacking and Data Breaches:

AI-driven systems are attractive targets for hackers due to the sensitive nature of the data they process. Cyberattacks, such as phishing, ransomware, and denial-of-service (DoS) attacks, can compromise the integrity of CE systems.

2. IoT Device Vulnerabilities:

IoT devices, which play a key role in tracking resources and monitoring conditions, often lack robust security features. Weak or default passwords, outdated firmware, and unencrypted communications make these devices susceptible to exploitation.

3. Insider Threats:

Employees or partners with access to sensitive data can intentionally or unintentionally cause security breaches. Insider threats are particularly challenging to detect and prevent, requiring comprehensive monitoring and access control measures.

Regulatory Compliance Challenges

1. Data Protection Laws:

Compliance with regulations such as the General Data Protection Regulation (GDPR) in Europe, the California Consumer Privacy Act (CCPA), and other regional data protection laws is essential for organizations leveraging AI in CE. These laws impose strict requirements for data handling, user consent, and breach notifications.

2. Cross-Border Data Transfers:

Circular supply chains often operate globally, necessitating the transfer of data across borders. Differences in regulatory frameworks between regions can create compliance challenges and expose organizations to legal risks.

3. Evolving Standards:

Data privacy and security standards continue to evolve as technologies and threats advance. Staying compliant requires organizations to monitor regulatory changes and adapt their systems accordingly.

Ethical Implications

1. Informed Consent:

Collecting and processing data without obtaining informed consent from individuals raises ethical concerns. Transparent communication about data collection practices and obtaining explicit user consent are critical for addressing these issues.

2. Data Minimization:

AI systems often collect more data than necessary for their intended purpose, increasing privacy risks. Implementing data minimization principles ensures that only essential information is collected and processed.

3. Bias in Data Usage:

Improper use of collected data can lead to biases in AI algorithms, resulting in unfair or discriminatory outcomes. Ethical frameworks are needed to guide the responsible use of data in CE applications.

Mitigating Privacy and Security Challenges

1. Robust Encryption:

Encrypting data at rest and in transit is a fundamental measure for protecting sensitive information. Advanced encryption standards

(AES) ensure that data remains secure even if intercepted or accessed without authorization.

2. Access Controls:

Implementing role-based access controls (RBAC) restricts data access to authorized personnel only. Multi-factor authentication (MFA) adds an additional layer of security, reducing the risk of unauthorized access.

3. Regular Audits:

Conducting regular security audits helps organizations identify vulnerabilities and implement corrective actions. Penetration testing and vulnerability assessments are particularly effective for evaluating system resilience.

4. Anonymization Techniques:

Anonymizing data before processing reduces privacy risks by removing personally identifiable information (PII). Techniques such as data masking and pseudonymization ensure that sensitive details remain protected.

5. Cybersecurity Training:

Educating employees and stakeholders about best practices for data security is essential for preventing breaches caused by human error. Training programs should cover topics such as password management, phishing awareness, and secure data handling.

Future Directions

Addressing privacy and data security challenges requires continuous innovation, collaboration, and adherence to ethical principles. As AI technologies advance, organizations must adopt proactive measures to mitigate risks, ensure compliance, and maintain trust in AI-driven CE systems. These efforts will support the development of resilient and sustainable supply chains while safeguarding the rights and interests of all stakeholders.

Addressing Biases in AI Algorithms for Equitable Outcomes

AI has the potential to transform the CE by driving efficiency and sustainability. However, biases in AI algorithms can undermine equitable outcomes, leading to unfair resource allocation, discriminatory decision-making, or unequal access to benefits. These biases can arise from data, design processes, or deployment practices. Addressing algorithmic biases is essential to ensure that AI systems used in the CE align with ethical principles and promote fairness for all stakeholders.

Understanding Bias in AI Algorithms

Bias in AI algorithms refers to systematic errors or skewed outcomes that disproportionately favor or disadvantage certain groups or entities. Biases can manifest in various ways, including:

1. **Data Bias:**

AI systems rely on training data to learn patterns and make decisions. If the training data is incomplete, unrepresentative, or reflects historical inequalities, the resulting algorithms may perpetuate or amplify these biases.

2. **Design Bias:**

Biases can be introduced during the development of AI systems if developers unconsciously embed their own assumptions or fail to consider diverse perspectives.

3. Deployment Bias:

The context in which AI systems are deployed can also lead to biased outcomes. For example, using AI in environments that lack inclusivity or equitable access can exacerbate disparities.

Impacts of Bias on Equitable Outcomes

In the context of the CE, biases in AI algorithms can have significant consequences:

1. Unequal Resource Allocation:

AI systems used for resource optimization or material recovery may prioritize certain regions, industries, or demographics over others, leading to unequal access to resources or services.

2. Discriminatory Practices:

Algorithms used for decision-making, such as selecting suppliers or designing waste management strategies, may inadvertently favor or disadvantage specific groups based on biased data.

3. Exclusion of Marginalized Communities:

If AI systems fail to consider the needs and circumstances of marginalized or underserved communities, these groups may be excluded from the benefits of CE initiatives.

Addressing Bias in AI Algorithms

1. Improving Data Quality and Representation:

Ensuring that training data is representative, accurate, and unbiased is critical for reducing algorithmic bias.

- **Diverse Data Collection:** Collect data from a wide range of sources to capture diverse perspectives and contexts. This includes incorporating data from underserved regions or communities that may have been overlooked in traditional datasets.

- **Auditing and Cleaning Data:** Regularly audit datasets for inaccuracies, missing information, or biases. Remove or correct biased data to improve the fairness of AI systems.

- **Synthetic Data Generation:** In cases where real-world data is limited, generate synthetic data to fill gaps and ensure that all relevant groups or scenarios are represented.

2. Embedding Ethical Principles in Design:

Ethical considerations should be integrated into the development of AI systems to mitigate biases and promote equitable outcomes.

- **Interdisciplinary Teams:** Assemble diverse development teams with varied backgrounds, expertise, and perspectives to identify and address potential biases during the design process.

- **Bias Mitigation Techniques:** Use ML techniques designed to reduce bias, such as fairness-aware algorithms or regularization methods that penalize discriminatory outcomes.

- **Transparency and Explainability:** Prioritize the development of explainable AI (XAI) systems that provide clear insights into decision-making processes, enabling stakeholders to identify and address potential biases.

3. Regular Monitoring and Evaluation:

Biases can emerge over time as AI systems are exposed to new data or used in different contexts. Ongoing monitoring and evaluation are essential for identifying and addressing these issues.

• **Bias Audits:** Conduct regular audits of AI algorithms to assess their performance and detect any unintended biases. Use fairness metrics to measure the impact of biases on different groups.

• **Feedback Loops:** Implement mechanisms for collecting user feedback to identify and address biases that may arise during deployment.

• **Adaptive Systems:** Design AI systems that can adapt and learn from new, unbiased data to improve their fairness over time.

4. Promoting Inclusivity in Deployment:

Ensure that AI systems are deployed in ways that promote inclusivity and equitable access to benefits.

• **Community Engagement:** Engage with local communities, stakeholders, and organizations to understand their needs and concerns. Incorporate their input into the deployment of AI systems.

• **Access to Technology:** Address barriers to technology access, such as cost or digital literacy, to ensure that underserved groups can benefit from AI-driven CE initiatives.

• **Localized Solutions:** Tailor AI solutions to the specific needs and contexts of different regions or communities to avoid one-size-fits-all approaches that may exacerbate disparities.

5. Establishing Governance Frameworks:

Strong governance frameworks are essential for ensuring accountability and fairness in AI systems.

• **Ethical Standards:** Adopt ethical standards and guidelines for AI development and deployment, focusing on fairness, transparency, and accountability.

• **Independent Oversight:** Establish independent oversight bodies to monitor the use of AI systems and investigate instances of bias or unfair outcomes.

• **Legal and Regulatory Compliance:** Ensure that AI systems comply with relevant laws and regulations, such as anti-discrimination or data protection laws.

Future Directions for Bias Mitigation

Addressing biases in AI algorithms is an ongoing process that requires collaboration, innovation, and vigilance. Emerging technologies, such as federated learning and privacy-preserving ML, offer new opportunities to reduce biases while protecting data privacy. By fostering interdisciplinary research, promoting ethical AI practices, and engaging with diverse stakeholders, organizations can create AI systems that advance the goals of the CE while ensuring equitable outcomes for all.

Policy and Governance Frameworks for AI in the Circular Economy

The integration of AI into CE practices requires robust policy and governance frameworks to ensure that these technologies are used responsibly, effectively, and equitably. Governance frameworks help establish clear guidelines for the ethical use of AI, manage risks, and align technological advancements with societal and environmental goals. These frameworks address issues such as data privacy, accountability, transparency, and fairness while promoting innovation and collaboration in AI-driven CE initiatives.

The Need for Policy and Governance in AI for CE

1. Ensuring Ethical Use:

AI systems in the CE involve decisions about resource allocation, material recovery, and waste management, which have far-reaching social and environmental impacts. Governance frameworks ensure that these decisions align with ethical principles and do not perpetuate harm or inequality.

2. Mitigating Risks:

The use of AI in CE introduces risks such as algorithmic bias, data breaches, and misuse of technology. Policies and governance frameworks are essential for mitigating these risks and ensuring that AI systems operate securely and fairly.

3. Driving Compliance and Accountability:

Governance frameworks establish accountability mechanisms to ensure compliance with regulations, standards, and best practices. This fosters trust among stakeholders and reduces the potential for misuse or unintended consequences.

Key Elements of Policy and Governance Frameworks

1. Ethical Guidelines:

Policies must incorporate ethical guidelines to govern the development and deployment of AI in CE. These guidelines should address principles such as fairness, transparency, accountability, and sustainability.

• **Fairness:** Ensure that AI systems are free from bias and promote equitable outcomes across communities and stakeholder groups.

• **Transparency:** Require that AI systems provide clear and explainable decision-making processes to stakeholders.

• **Accountability:** Define roles and responsibilities for AI developers, operators, and users to address potential failures or unethical practices.

2. Data Governance:

Effective data governance policies are critical for managing the vast amounts of data used by AI systems in CE.

• **Privacy Protections:** Enforce data privacy regulations, such as GDPR, to safeguard personal and sensitive information.

• **Data Standards:** Establish standards for data quality, interoperability, and sharing to ensure that AI systems operate efficiently and securely.

• **Data Access:** Promote equitable access to data while maintaining security and compliance with privacy laws.

3. Regulatory Compliance:

Policies must ensure that AI systems comply with relevant laws and regulations governing CE practices, such as waste management directives, environmental protection laws, and anti-discrimination regulations.

• **Cross-Border Compliance:** Address challenges related to the global nature of supply chains by harmonizing regulations across jurisdictions.

• **Sector-Specific Rules:** Develop tailored policies for different sectors, such as manufacturing, transportation, or agriculture, to address their unique challenges and opportunities in the CE.

4. Risk Management:

Governance frameworks should include mechanisms for identifying, assessing, and mitigating risks associated with AI in CE.

• **Impact Assessments:** Conduct regular assessments of the environmental, social, and economic impacts of AI systems.

• **Risk Mitigation Plans:** Develop contingency plans to address potential failures, cyberattacks, or other disruptions.

5. Collaboration and Stakeholder Engagement:

Effective governance frameworks promote collaboration among stakeholders, including governments, businesses, academia, and civil society.

• **Public-Private Partnerships:** Foster partnerships between public and private entities to drive innovation and share resources for AI-driven CE initiatives.

• **Community Involvement:** Engage local communities in decision-making processes to ensure that AI systems meet their needs and address potential concerns.

Global and Regional Frameworks

1. International Standards:

Organizations such as the United Nations and the World Economic Forum are developing global standards for AI governance. These frameworks aim to harmonize regulations and promote best practices across countries.

• **UN AI Ethics Guidelines:** Provide overarching principles for ethical AI use, including inclusivity, transparency, and sustainability.

• **OECD AI Principles:** Offer recommendations for fostering trust and promoting the responsible development of AI technologies.

2. Regional Policies:

Regional policies, such as the European Union's CE Action Plan and the AI Act, integrate CE and AI considerations to address unique local challenges.

• **EU AI Act:** Establishes rules for AI applications, including requirements for high-risk systems and transparency obligations.

• **Asia-Pacific Policies:** Focus on promoting AI-driven innovation while addressing environmental and social challenges specific to the region.

3. National Strategies:

Countries are adopting national strategies to regulate AI use in CE, with a focus on aligning technological advancements with sustainability goals.

• **Green AI Initiatives:** Encourage the development of energy-efficient AI systems to minimize their environmental footprint.

• **Incentive Programs:** Provide funding and tax benefits for businesses implementing AI in CE practices.

Accountability Mechanisms

1. Independent Oversight Bodies:

Establish independent agencies to monitor and enforce compliance with governance frameworks. These bodies can investigate complaints, conduct audits, and impose penalties for violations.

2. Audit and Reporting Requirements:

Require organizations to conduct regular audits of their AI systems and publish reports on their environmental and social impacts. This fosters transparency and accountability.

3. Redress Mechanisms:

Provide stakeholders with mechanisms to report grievances or seek redress in cases of harm caused by AI systems.

Future Directions for Policy and Governance

1. Dynamic Frameworks:

Governance frameworks must evolve to keep pace with advancements in AI and changing societal expectations. Regular reviews and updates ensure that policies remain relevant and effective.

2. Cross-Sector Collaboration:

Strengthen partnerships across sectors to share knowledge, resources, and best practices for AI governance in CE.

3. Education and Capacity Building:

Invest in education and training programs to build awareness and expertise in AI governance among policymakers, businesses, and communities.

By implementing robust policy and governance frameworks, stakeholders can ensure that AI technologies are harnessed responsibly to advance the goals of the CE, fostering sustainable and equitable outcomes for all.

Chapter 8: Future Directions and Innovations

The integration of AI into the CE is rapidly evolving, opening new possibilities for innovation and sustainable practices. Future advancements in AI technology, combined with emerging trends such as digital twins, blockchain, and advanced robotics, promise to revolutionize how resources are managed, waste is minimized, and systems are optimized. This chapter explores potential breakthroughs and innovative applications of AI that could drive the next phase of the CE. By examining these future directions, we highlight opportunities to accelerate sustainability, enhance collaboration, and address global challenges in resource management.

Emerging AI Technologies for the Circular Economy

The CE seeks to reduce waste and maximize the value of resources through reuse, recycling, and regeneration. AI plays a critical role in enabling this transition, and emerging AI technologies are set to enhance the efficiency, scalability, and innovation of CE practices. These technologies, including advanced ML models, digital twins, and federated learning, provide new opportunities to optimize resource use, improve waste management, and create sustainable systems.

Advanced Machine Learning Models

ML is a cornerstone of AI, and advancements in ML models are unlocking new potential for CE applications.

1. Deep Reinforcement Learning:

Deep reinforcement learning combines reinforcement learning with neural networks to make complex decisions in dynamic environments. For example, it can optimize material flows in real time by learning from changing conditions, such as fluctuations in resource availability or demand.

2. Transfer Learning:

Transfer learning enables AI models trained on one task to adapt to related tasks, reducing the need for extensive data. In the CE, this technology allows algorithms to be reused across different industries or regions, accelerating the deployment of AI-driven solutions in areas such as waste sorting or resource optimization.

3. Explainable AI (XAI):

Explainable AI enhances the interpretability of ML models, enabling stakeholders to understand how decisions are made. In CE applications, XAI ensures transparency in areas like material selection or recycling recommendations, fostering trust and accountability.

Digital Twins

Digital twins are virtual replicas of physical assets, processes, or systems that provide real-time insights and predictive capabilities. These AI-enabled models are transforming CE by improving resource tracking, operational efficiency, and decision-making.

1. Resource Flow Optimization:

Digital twins simulate resource flows across supply chains, identifying inefficiencies and suggesting improvements. For instance, they can predict bottlenecks in reverse logistics systems, enabling businesses to address issues before they escalate.

2. Lifecycle Analysis:

By modeling the entire lifecycle of products, digital twins help organizations assess environmental impacts and identify opportunities for circular practices, such as design changes to enhance durability or recyclability.

3. Dynamic Decision Support:

Digital twins provide real-time data and predictive analytics to support decision-making in CE systems. For example, they can recommend optimal recycling methods based on the composition and condition of materials.

Federated Learning

Federated learning is an emerging AI approach that enables decentralized model training without sharing raw data. This technology is particularly valuable for CE applications involving sensitive or proprietary information.

1. Collaborative Innovation:

Federated learning allows multiple organizations to collaborate on AI model development while maintaining data privacy. This fosters innovation in areas like waste management or material recovery, where data sharing is often limited by competitive concerns.

2. Data Privacy and Security:

By processing data locally and sharing only model updates, federated learning reduces privacy risks. This is crucial for CE applications that involve consumer data, such as usage patterns in sharing platforms or subscription services.

3. Scalability Across Regions:

Federated learning enables AI models to be trained on diverse datasets from different regions, improving their accuracy and applicability across various CE contexts.

AI-Enabled Robotics

Robotics powered by AI is advancing rapidly, providing new capabilities for automation and precision in CE operations.

1. Autonomous Sorting Systems:

AI-driven robots equipped with computer vision can sort waste materials with high accuracy, distinguishing between different types of plastics, metals, and textiles. This improves the efficiency and quality of recycling processes.

2. Disassembly Robots:

Robotics systems are being developed to disassemble complex products, such as electronics or vehicles, into their component parts for reuse or recycling. These systems reduce labor costs and improve material recovery rates.

3. On-Site Waste Processing:

Autonomous robots enable on-site processing of waste materials, such as shredding or compacting, reducing transportation costs and emissions. This technology is particularly useful for remote or underserved areas.

Generative AI for Design Innovation

Generative AI uses algorithms to create novel designs or solutions, making it a powerful tool for sustainable product development.

1. Material Efficiency:

Generative AI optimizes product designs for material efficiency, reducing waste during production. For example, it can suggest lightweight structures that maintain strength and durability.

2. Modular Design:

Generative algorithms support the creation of modular products that are easier to repair, upgrade, or recycle, aligning with CE principles.

3. Sustainability Trade-Offs:

Generative AI evaluates trade-offs between environmental, economic, and functional factors, helping designers make informed decisions that prioritize sustainability.

Blockchain-Integrated AI

The combination of AI and blockchain technology enhances transparency and accountability in CE systems.

1. Traceability Solutions:

Blockchain records material origins and lifecycle data, while AI analyzes this information to optimize recycling, reuse, and recovery processes.

2. Fraud Detection:

AI-powered algorithms identify inconsistencies in blockchain records, ensuring the authenticity of data and preventing fraud in CE supply chains.

3. Incentive Mechanisms:

Blockchain-integrated AI supports systems that incentivize circular practices, such as rewarding consumers for returning used products or recycling materials.

Real-Time Edge AI

Edge AI processes data locally on devices rather than relying on cloud infrastructure, enabling faster and more efficient decision-making in CE applications.

1. Energy Efficiency:

Edge AI reduces energy consumption by minimizing data transmission and processing requirements, making it a sustainable choice for CE systems.

2. IoT Integration:

Edge AI enhances IoT devices by enabling real-time analysis of sensor data, improving monitoring and management of resources across supply chains.

3. On-Site Decision-Making:

Edge AI supports localized decision-making, such as optimizing resource allocation or identifying material recovery opportunities in real time.

Future Potential

Emerging AI technologies continue to push the boundaries of what is possible in the CE. By integrating these innovations into CE systems, organizations can enhance efficiency, scalability, and sustainability, creating a future where resources are managed responsibly and waste is minimized. Overcoming challenges such as implementation costs, data integration, and skill gaps will be essential for realizing the full potential of these technologies.

Integration of AI with Other Digital Technologies (e.g., IoT, Blockchain)

The integration of AI with other digital technologies, such as the IoT and blockchain, is transforming how the CE operates. These combined technologies create intelligent systems that improve efficiency, transparency, and scalability in resource management, waste reduction, and supply chain operations. By leveraging AI alongside IoT and blockchain, organizations can build interconnected ecosystems that support the principles of CE, driving innovation and sustainability.

AI and IoT Integration

IoT refers to the network of connected devices and sensors that collect and exchange data in real time. When combined with AI, IoT systems become more intelligent and capable of analyzing vast amounts of data to inform decisions and optimize processes.

1. **Real-Time Monitoring and Analytics:**

IoT devices embedded in products, packaging, or infrastructure collect data on parameters such as location, temperature, and usage. AI analyzes this data in real time, providing actionable insights for CE applications. For example, AI-driven IoT systems can monitor the condition of recyclable materials, ensuring they are collected and processed at the optimal time.

2. **Predictive Maintenance:**

IoT-enabled sensors monitor equipment performance, while AI predicts maintenance needs based on usage patterns and historical data. This reduces downtime, extends equipment lifespans, and minimizes waste, aligning with CE goals.

3. Dynamic Resource Allocation:

AI-powered IoT systems optimize resource allocation by analyzing real-time data on supply and demand. For instance, shared mobility services use AI and IoT to allocate vehicles to high-demand areas, reducing idle time and maximizing resource utilization.

4. Environmental Monitoring:

IoT devices track environmental factors such as air quality, water usage, and waste generation. AI processes this data to identify inefficiencies and recommend improvements, promoting sustainability in industrial and urban environments.

AI and Blockchain Integration

Blockchain is a decentralized and immutable digital ledger that ensures transparency and security in data transactions. Integrating AI with blockchain enhances data integrity, traceability, and decision-making in CE systems.

1. Traceability and Provenance:

Blockchain records the origin and lifecycle of materials, while AI analyzes this information to identify opportunities for recycling, reuse, or refurbishment. For example, in the fashion industry, AI and blockchain track the lifecycle of textiles, ensuring compliance with sustainability standards and enabling the recovery of materials at the end of their life.

2. Fraud Prevention:

Blockchain ensures the authenticity of data, and AI algorithms detect inconsistencies or anomalies in blockchain records. This prevents fraud and ensures that information related to resource flows and CE practices is reliable.

3. Smart Contracts:

AI enhances blockchain-based smart contracts by automating complex processes and decision-making. For example, in CE supply chains, smart contracts can trigger payments or material transfers based on AI-analyzed data, reducing administrative burdens and improving efficiency.

4. Incentivizing Circular Practices:

Blockchain-integrated AI supports systems that reward individuals or businesses for participating in circular practices. For instance, consumers could earn tokens for returning used products or recycling materials, with AI tracking and validating these activities.

AI, IoT, and Blockchain Synergies

The combination of AI, IoT, and blockchain creates powerful synergies that enhance CE operations across industries. Together, these technologies enable intelligent, transparent, and scalable systems.

1. Closed-Loop Supply Chains:

IoT devices track materials throughout their lifecycle, blockchain ensures data transparency, and AI optimizes material recovery and reuse. These technologies work together to create closed-loop supply chains that minimize waste and maximize resource value.

2. Dynamic Inventory Management:

IoT sensors monitor inventory levels, blockchain provides a secure record of transactions, and AI predicts demand and restocking needs. This integration reduces overproduction, waste, and inefficiencies in supply chains.

3. Enhanced Recycling Systems:

IoT devices in waste collection bins provide data on material composition, blockchain records the recycling process, and AI analyzes the data to optimize recycling operations. This integration improves material recovery rates and reduces contamination.

4. Real-Time Decision-Making:

AI processes data from IoT devices in real time, while blockchain ensures the integrity of the data. This enables organizations to make informed decisions quickly, such as redirecting resources to high-demand areas or adjusting production schedules based on material availability.

Challenges in Integration

While the integration of AI with IoT and blockchain offers significant benefits, it also presents challenges that must be addressed:

1. Data Interoperability:

Integrating data from diverse sources requires standardized formats and protocols. Ensuring interoperability between AI, IoT, and blockchain systems is essential for seamless operation.

2. High Implementation Costs:

Deploying AI, IoT, and blockchain technologies involves significant upfront investments in hardware, software, and infrastructure. Businesses must weigh these costs against long-term benefits.

3. Scalability Issues:

Scaling integrated systems across global supply chains or large organizations requires robust infrastructure and expertise. Overcoming these challenges is critical for widespread adoption.

4. Data Privacy and Security:

Sharing data across IoT, blockchain, and AI systems increases the risk of breaches or unauthorized access. Implementing strong encryption and access controls is vital for safeguarding sensitive information.

Future Opportunities

The integration of AI with IoT and blockchain is poised to unlock new opportunities for CE applications:

1. Digital Twins:

Combining IoT data with AI and blockchain can create digital twins of supply chains or products, enabling advanced simulations and optimization.

2. Decentralized AI Models:

Blockchain can support decentralized AI models, allowing multiple organizations to collaborate on AI-driven CE solutions while maintaining data privacy.

3. Edge AI Systems:

IoT devices equipped with edge AI capabilities can process data locally, reducing latency and improving real-time decision-making in CE operations.

By addressing challenges and leveraging synergies, the integration of AI, IoT, and blockchain has the potential to revolutionize the CE, creating smarter, more efficient, and sustainable systems.

Scaling AI Solutions for Global Resource Challenges

The world faces pressing resource challenges, including finite natural resources, escalating waste, and environmental degradation. AI offers transformative solutions for addressing these issues through enhanced resource efficiency, waste minimization, and sustainable practices. However, scaling AI solutions to tackle these global challenges requires overcoming technological, organizational, financial, and regulatory hurdles. By addressing these barriers, AI can play a central role in managing resources more effectively on a global scale, fostering a sustainable future.

The Importance of Scaling AI for Global Resource Challenges

Scaling AI solutions enables their deployment across industries, geographies, and supply chains, amplifying their impact. Key benefits of scaling AI include:

1. Enhanced Resource Efficiency:

AI optimizes the use of resources by improving processes such as material flow, inventory management, and demand forecasting. Scaling these solutions can significantly reduce resource wastage on a global level.

2. Accelerated CE Transition:

Scaled AI systems enable widespread adoption of CE practices, such as recycling, remanufacturing, and product lifecycle analysis, promoting sustainability across sectors.

3. Global Collaboration:

Scaling AI fosters collaboration among countries, industries, and organizations to address shared resource challenges, driving collective progress toward sustainability goals.

Challenges in Scaling AI Solutions

1. Technological Barriers:

Scaling AI requires robust digital infrastructure, advanced computing power, and seamless data integration. Many regions, particularly developing countries, lack the necessary technological infrastructure to support AI systems.

2. Data Accessibility and Quality:

Effective AI solutions rely on high-quality, diverse datasets. Limited access to reliable data, particularly in underserved regions, poses a significant challenge to scaling AI globally.

3. High Implementation Costs:

Scaling AI solutions involves significant financial investment in hardware, software, training, and maintenance. These costs can be prohibitive for SMEs or organizations in developing economies.

4. Skill Gaps:

The deployment and scaling of AI require expertise in data science, ML, and AI development. The global shortage of skilled professionals in these fields creates a bottleneck for scaling efforts.

5. Regulatory Complexity:

Navigating diverse regulatory frameworks across countries and industries complicates the scaling of AI solutions. Variations in data privacy laws, environmental regulations, and intellectual property rights create additional hurdles.

Strategies for Scaling AI Solutions

1. Investing in Infrastructure:

Building the necessary digital and physical infrastructure is critical for scaling AI solutions.

• **Cloud Computing:** Leveraging cloud-based platforms enables organizations to access scalable computing resources without significant upfront investment.

• **IoT Deployment:** Expanding IoT networks supports data collection at scale, enabling AI systems to operate effectively across diverse environments.

• **Digital Inclusion:** Governments and international organizations must prioritize investments in digital infrastructure, particularly in developing regions, to bridge the digital divide.

2. Fostering Collaboration:

Collaboration among stakeholders accelerates the scaling of AI solutions.

• **Public-Private Partnerships:** Partnerships between governments, businesses, and academic institutions can pool resources, share knowledge, and drive innovation in AI applications for resource management.

• **Global Alliances:** International alliances, such as the United Nations Sustainable Development Goals (SDGs), provide a framework for scaling AI solutions to address global challenges collectively.

3. Improving Data Access and Sharing:

Addressing data-related challenges is essential for scaling AI.

• **Open Data Initiatives:** Encouraging open data policies and platforms promotes data sharing among organizations, enabling AI systems to learn from diverse datasets.

• **Standardization:** Developing standardized data formats and protocols ensures compatibility across systems and regions, facilitating seamless data integration.

4. Developing Cost-Effective Solutions:

Reducing the financial barriers to AI adoption supports scaling efforts.

• **AI-as-a-Service Models:** Cloud-based AI services lower the cost of entry for organizations by providing scalable, pay-as-you-go solutions.

• **Subsidies and Incentives:** Governments can offer financial incentives, such as tax breaks or grants, to encourage businesses to adopt and scale AI technologies.

5. Building Capacity:

Addressing skill gaps through education and training is critical for scaling AI solutions.

• **Workforce Development:** Investing in training programs, certifications, and higher education in AI and data science equips workers with the skills needed to implement and manage AI systems.

• **Knowledge Transfer:** Partnerships between developed and developing regions can facilitate the transfer of knowledge and expertise, supporting global capacity-building efforts.

6. Navigating Regulatory Landscapes:

Harmonizing regulations across borders and industries simplifies the scaling of AI.

• **International Standards:** Developing global standards for AI governance, data privacy, and sustainability ensures consistency and compliance.

• **Regulatory Sandboxes:** Governments can establish regulatory sandboxes to test and refine AI applications in a controlled environment, reducing barriers to adoption.

Opportunities for Global Impact

1. Sustainable Agriculture:

Scaled AI solutions can optimize agricultural practices by predicting weather patterns, managing water usage, and improving crop yields. This helps address global food security challenges while minimizing resource consumption.

2. Energy Efficiency:

AI-driven energy management systems can be scaled to optimize energy usage in buildings, industries, and transportation, reducing greenhouse gas emissions and promoting renewable energy adoption.

3. Waste Management:

Scaling AI-enabled waste sorting and recycling systems improves material recovery rates and reduces environmental pollution, advancing the goals of the CE.

4. Urban Planning:

AI solutions can support sustainable urban development by optimizing traffic flows, managing resources, and reducing energy consumption in cities.

5. Disaster Resilience:

Scaled AI systems enhance disaster prediction and response, enabling communities to prepare for and recover from resource-related crises more effectively.

Future Directions

The successful scaling of AI solutions for global resource challenges requires sustained investment, collaboration, and innovation. By addressing existing barriers and leveraging opportunities, AI has the potential to revolutionize resource management on a global scale, creating a sustainable and equitable future for all. Governments, businesses, and civil society must work together to realize the full potential of AI in solving the world's most pressing resource challenges.

Vision for the Future: AI Enabling a Global Circular Economy

The CE represents a transformative shift from the traditional linear model of production and consumption toward a sustainable system that minimizes waste and maximizes resource efficiency. AI has the potential to drive this transition on a global scale, offering advanced tools to optimize processes, enhance decision-making, and promote sustainability across industries and geographies. A future enabled by AI envisions a fully interconnected, efficient, and resilient CE that addresses global challenges while fostering innovation and inclusivity.

Global Resource Efficiency

1. Optimized Resource Use:

AI can revolutionize resource management by analyzing vast datasets to optimize material flows, reduce inefficiencies, and minimize waste. Advanced algorithms will enable industries to make data-driven decisions that prioritize resource conservation while maintaining productivity and profitability.

2. Predictive Capabilities:

In the future, AI systems will integrate predictive analytics to anticipate demand, supply chain disruptions, and resource shortages. These capabilities will allow businesses to respond proactively, ensuring stability in global supply chains and reducing overproduction and waste.

3. Intelligent Design:

AI-powered generative design tools will facilitate the creation of products that are modular, repairable, and recyclable. This will ensure that resources remain in circulation longer, aligning with CE principles and reducing the need for virgin material extraction.

Enhanced Circular Supply Chains

1. Real-Time Transparency:

AI will enable global supply chains to achieve complete transparency through real-time monitoring and tracking of resources. IoT devices and blockchain technology will integrate with AI systems to provide accurate, verifiable data on the lifecycle of materials, fostering trust and accountability.

2. Closed-Loop Systems:

Future AI applications will fully support closed-loop supply chains by optimizing reverse logistics, enabling the recovery and reintegration of materials into production cycles. This will create a seamless flow of resources, reducing waste and supporting CE goals.

3. Decentralized Networks:

AI-driven platforms will facilitate decentralized supply chains that are resilient to disruptions. By leveraging local resource recovery and production capabilities, these networks will reduce transportation emissions and foster regional sustainability.

Scaling Global Collaboration

1. Unified Frameworks:

AI will play a key role in developing unified frameworks for CE practices that can be adopted globally. Standardized systems and data-sharing protocols will allow industries across regions to collaborate effectively, driving collective progress toward sustainability goals.

2. Cross-Sector Partnerships:

AI-enabled platforms will foster partnerships between industries, governments, and non-profits to address shared challenges. These collaborations will result in innovative solutions that leverage AI to tackle resource inefficiencies and environmental degradation.

3. Inclusive Participation:

Future AI systems will prioritize inclusivity, ensuring that all stakeholders, including marginalized communities, have access to the benefits of a global CE. By tailoring solutions to regional contexts and providing equitable access to technologies, AI will support a fair and just transition.

Waste-Free Societies

1. Advanced Waste Management:

AI will transform waste management by automating sorting and processing operations, ensuring that materials are recovered efficiently and directed to appropriate recycling or reuse streams. This will significantly reduce landfill dependency and environmental pollution.

2. Zero-Waste Cities:

Urban areas will leverage AI to become zero-waste cities, where every material is tracked, collected, and reintegrated into production cycles. AI-powered systems will optimize resource recovery at both the household and industrial levels, promoting sustainable urban living.

3. Consumer Empowerment:

AI-driven applications will educate and empower consumers to make sustainable choices. From recommending eco-friendly products to providing insights on reducing waste, these tools will foster a culture of environmental responsibility.

Accelerating Innovation

1. Emerging Technologies:

The integration of AI with emerging technologies, such as digital twins, federated learning, and edge computing, will create powerful systems for resource management and waste reduction. These advancements will drive CE innovation across industries.

2. AI-Driven Business Models:

New business models, such as product-as-a-service and sharing platforms, will be enabled by AI systems that optimize asset usage and track performance. These models will reduce resource consumption while creating economic opportunities.

3. Continuous Learning Systems:

Future AI applications will incorporate continuous learning capabilities, allowing them to adapt to changing conditions and improve over time. This will ensure that CE practices remain relevant and effective in addressing global challenges.

Addressing Global Challenges

1. Climate Resilience:

AI will enable CE systems to contribute to climate resilience by reducing greenhouse gas emissions, optimizing renewable energy usage, and supporting carbon sequestration efforts. These contributions will mitigate the impacts of climate change while fostering sustainability.

2. Resource Scarcity:

By promoting efficient use and recovery of resources, AI will address the growing issue of resource scarcity, ensuring that essential materials remain available for future generations.

3. Economic Growth:

The global adoption of AI-driven CE systems will create new economic opportunities, from green jobs to innovative markets for secondary materials. These systems will foster sustainable economic growth while reducing environmental impacts.

A Shared Vision for the Future

The future of AI-enabled CE is one of global collaboration, innovation, and sustainability. By addressing existing barriers and leveraging emerging technologies, AI has the potential to create a world where resources are managed responsibly, waste is eliminated, and societies thrive within planetary boundaries. Governments, businesses, and individuals must work together to realize this vision, ensuring that AI serves as a catalyst for a sustainable and inclusive global CE.

Conclusion

As the CE emerges as a critical framework for addressing global sustainability challenges, the role of AI in advancing its principles cannot be overstated. Throughout this book, we have explored how AI enables innovative approaches to resource efficiency, waste reduction, and the optimization of supply chains. In this concluding chapter, we reflect on the key insights and themes discussed, emphasize the importance of aligning AI-driven solutions with ethical and governance frameworks, and envision the path forward for integrating AI into a global CE. This chapter serves as a call to action for stakeholders to embrace the potential of AI while addressing its challenges to create a sustainable, equitable future.

Summary of Key Insights from Each Chapter

The integration of AI into the CE offers transformative potential for resource efficiency, waste reduction, and sustainability. This book provided a comprehensive exploration of how AI supports and advances CE principles, with each chapter focusing on specific aspects and opportunities.

Introduction

The introduction outlined the urgent need for transitioning to a CE to address global resource challenges, emphasizing AI's role as a powerful enabler. It highlighted the foundational concepts of CE and AI, the synergies between them, and the structure of the book to guide readers through this complex, interconnected topic.

Chapter 1: Foundations of the Circular Economy and AI

This chapter established the principles and benefits of CE, such as reducing waste, maximizing resource utility, and minimizing environmental impact. It introduced key AI concepts and applications, demonstrating how technologies like ML and predictive analytics can optimize circular systems. The intersection of AI and CE was explored, identifying synergies and opportunities, as well as challenges in integrating these domains.

Chapter 2: AI in Resource Optimization

This chapter focused on how AI supports efficient resource use, including mapping and tracking resources, forecasting demand, and optimizing material flows. ML algorithms and predictive analytics were presented as critical tools for minimizing resource waste and ensuring sustainable operations. It also addressed limitations and barriers in implementing AI-driven resource optimization solutions.

Chapter 3: AI for Waste Minimization

AI's role in waste minimization was examined, particularly in identifying and classifying waste, designing waste-free manufacturing processes, and enhancing recycling and remanufacturing systems. The chapter emphasized AI's ability to create a zero-waste future by supporting innovative solutions and real-time decision-making.

Chapter 4: AI in Sustainable Product Design

This chapter explored how AI-driven tools enable lifecycle analysis, material selection, and generative design for sustainable products. AI technologies were shown to promote modularity, durability, and repairability in product design, aligning with CE principles and reducing environmental impacts.

Chapter 5: AI-Driven Business Models in the Circular Economy

AI-powered business models, such as sharing platforms, subscription services, and circular supply chains, were discussed in this chapter. AI's ability to optimize these models through predictive analytics and smart contracts was highlighted as a means to scale CE practices across industries.

Chapter 6: AI and Circular Supply Chains

The role of AI in creating efficient, transparent, and scalable circular supply chains was examined. Key applications included material tracking, reverse logistics optimization, and integration with blockchain and IoT. Challenges in implementing AI-driven supply chains were also addressed.

Chapter 7: Ethical and Governance Considerations

This chapter emphasized the importance of ethical AI practices and robust governance frameworks in CE applications. It addressed challenges such as bias, transparency, accountability, and data privacy, proposing strategies to ensure AI aligns with societal and environmental goals.

Chapter 8: Future Directions and Innovations

The final thematic chapter explored emerging AI technologies, including digital twins, federated learning, and generative design, that are poised to revolutionize CE practices. It discussed the potential for these innovations to accelerate global sustainability efforts and overcome existing barriers.

These insights collectively illustrate AI's transformative potential to drive the transition to a global CE, providing actionable strategies and a vision for the future.

The Transformative Potential of AI in the Circular Economy

AI holds transformative potential for advancing the CE, providing innovative solutions to optimize resource efficiency, minimize waste, and create sustainable systems. By leveraging technologies such as ML, predictive analytics, and real-time data processing, AI addresses many of the challenges associated with transitioning from a linear to a circular model of production and consumption.

Enhancing Resource Efficiency

AI optimizes resource use by analyzing vast amounts of data to identify inefficiencies, predict demand, and ensure the optimal allocation of materials. ML algorithms forecast consumption patterns, enabling businesses to adjust production schedules and inventory levels in real time. This reduces overproduction, eliminates excess waste, and conserves resources, aligning with CE principles. AI-powered tools also facilitate lifecycle analysis, allowing organizations to design products with durability, repairability, and recyclability in mind, extending the lifespan of materials.

Revolutionizing Waste Management

AI plays a critical role in transforming waste management systems, making them more efficient and effective. Advanced image recognition and computer vision technologies enable AI-powered sorting systems to identify and categorize waste materials with high precision. These systems improve recycling rates and reduce contamination, ensuring that valuable resources are recovered and reintegrated into production cycles. Additionally, AI-driven predictive maintenance systems prevent equipment failures, reducing industrial waste and extending the lifecycle of machinery.

Facilitating Sustainable Product Design

Generative design, powered by AI, allows businesses to create innovative products that minimize material use while maintaining functionality. These tools explore thousands of design permutations, optimizing for criteria such as material efficiency, durability, and environmental impact. AI also supports modular and repairable product designs, which enhance product longevity and ease of recycling, contributing to CE objectives. By integrating sustainability considerations into the design phase, AI enables organizations to align their products with CE principles from the outset.

Transforming Business Models

AI enables the development of new business models that support the CE, such as sharing platforms, subscription services, and product-as-a-service models. Predictive analytics help businesses manage asset performance, reduce downtime, and optimize usage, making these models viable and profitable. Smart contracts powered by AI and blockchain streamline operations by automating processes like payment settlements, material tracking, and performance monitoring, reducing administrative burdens and enhancing transparency.

Enabling Circular Supply Chains

AI improves circular supply chains by enhancing transparency, optimizing logistics, and enabling real-time decision-making. IoT devices collect data on material flows, while AI analyzes this data to track resources across their lifecycle. This visibility allows organizations to implement closed-loop systems, ensuring that materials are recovered, reused, and recycled efficiently. AI also facilitates the integration of blockchain technology, creating secure and immutable records of resource transactions, fostering trust among stakeholders.

Overcoming Global Challenges

The scalability of AI-driven solutions makes them instrumental in addressing global resource challenges. By automating complex processes and enabling collaboration across regions and industries, AI ensures the efficient management of limited resources.

Furthermore, AI supports climate resilience by reducing emissions, optimizing energy use, and mitigating environmental degradation.

The transformative potential of AI in the CE lies in its ability to drive innovation, efficiency, and sustainability across all stages of production and consumption. By integrating AI into CE practices, businesses and societies can accelerate the transition to a more sustainable and resilient future.

Challenges and Pathways for Implementation

The integration of AI into the CE holds immense potential to drive resource efficiency, waste reduction, and sustainability. However, implementing AI-driven solutions in CE systems is not without challenges. These barriers span technological, financial, organizational, and regulatory domains. Addressing these challenges requires strategic pathways that leverage innovation, collaboration, and policy support to ensure the successful adoption of AI in CE practices.

Technological Challenges

One of the primary challenges in implementing AI for the CE is the lack of technological infrastructure in many regions. Advanced AI systems rely on robust computing power, reliable internet connectivity, and seamless integration with other technologies like IoT and blockchain. Inadequate infrastructure limits the scalability of AI solutions, particularly in developing economies. Additionally, the complexity of AI models poses challenges for organizations with limited technical expertise. Developing and maintaining these systems requires highly skilled personnel and ongoing investment in technology upgrades.

Data availability and quality are critical factors for AI implementation. AI systems require vast amounts of accurate, diverse, and up-to-date data to function effectively. However, data silos, inconsistencies, and incomplete datasets often hinder the deployment of AI solutions. The absence of standardized data formats and protocols further complicates data integration, reducing the effectiveness of AI-driven CE systems.

Financial Barriers

The high costs associated with deploying AI solutions can deter organizations from adopting them. These costs include initial investments in hardware and software, training personnel, and maintaining systems over time. SMEs, which form a significant portion of global industries, often lack the financial resources to implement AI at scale. Moreover, demonstrating a return on investment (ROI) in the short term can be challenging, as the benefits of AI-driven CE systems are often realized over the long term.

Organizational Resistance

Implementing AI in CE systems requires a cultural shift within organizations. Resistance to change, particularly in industries with established linear models, can slow down adoption. Employees may fear job displacement due to automation, while stakeholders may be skeptical about the reliability and benefits of AI-driven processes. A lack of alignment between organizational goals and sustainability initiatives further exacerbates these challenges.

Regulatory and Ethical Issues

The absence of clear and consistent regulatory frameworks for AI and CE creates uncertainties for businesses. Navigating diverse regulations across regions, particularly concerning data privacy, intellectual property, and environmental standards, complicates implementation efforts. Ethical considerations, such as bias in AI algorithms and potential misuse of technology, also pose significant challenges that must be addressed to build trust and ensure equitable outcomes.

Pathways for Implementation

To overcome these challenges, organizations must adopt strategic pathways:

1. **Investing in Infrastructure:** Governments and industries must prioritize investments in digital infrastructure, such as high-speed internet, cloud computing, and IoT networks, to support AI deployment in CE systems.

2. **Fostering Collaboration:** Partnerships between public and private sectors, academic institutions, and international organizations can accelerate innovation, share resources, and drive collective action.

3. **Improving Data Management:** Establishing standardized data protocols, promoting open data initiatives, and leveraging advanced data cleaning and integration tools will enhance data quality and availability.

4. **Offering Financial Support:** Governments can provide subsidies, tax incentives, and grants to lower the financial barriers for businesses adopting AI-driven CE practices.

5. **Building Workforce Capacity:** Comprehensive training programs and upskilling initiatives will equip workers with the knowledge and skills required for AI implementation.

6. **Establishing Regulatory Frameworks:** Developing clear, consistent, and globally aligned regulations for AI and CE will create a stable environment for innovation.

7. **Promoting Ethical AI:** Organizations must prioritize fairness, transparency, and accountability in AI systems to address ethical concerns and build stakeholder trust.

By addressing these challenges and following these pathways, the integration of AI into the CE can be accelerated, unlocking its transformative potential to create sustainable and resilient systems.

Call to Action for Stakeholders: Governments, Businesses, and Society

The transition to a CE enabled by AI requires collective action from governments, businesses, and society. Each stakeholder group plays a crucial role in fostering the adoption and scaling of AI-driven solutions to address global resource challenges, reduce waste, and promote sustainability. To achieve these goals, coordinated efforts and commitments are essential to overcome barriers, drive innovation, and create a future aligned with the principles of CE.

Governments: Leading Through Policy and Infrastructure

Governments must take the lead in creating an enabling environment for the integration of AI in CE systems. Policy frameworks, financial incentives, and infrastructure development are key areas where governments can have a transformative impact.

1. **Policy Frameworks:**

Governments must establish clear, consistent, and globally aligned regulations to guide the ethical and sustainable use of AI in CE practices. Policies should address data privacy, AI accountability, and environmental standards, ensuring businesses operate within a secure and fair regulatory environment.

2. **Incentives for Adoption:**

Offering tax breaks, grants, and subsidies for organizations implementing AI-driven CE solutions can lower financial barriers and encourage widespread adoption. Governments can also support research and development initiatives to accelerate technological innovation.

3. Infrastructure Investment:

Governments should prioritize investments in digital infrastructure, including high-speed internet, cloud computing, and IoT networks, to enable the deployment of AI systems. These investments are particularly important in underserved regions to bridge the digital divide and ensure equitable access to AI technologies.

4. Public Awareness Campaigns:

Governments can promote the benefits of AI and CE through public awareness campaigns, encouraging societal participation and support for sustainable practices.

Businesses: Driving Innovation and Adoption

Businesses are at the forefront of implementing AI solutions in CE systems, leveraging innovation to optimize operations and deliver sustainable outcomes.

1. Investing in AI and CE Integration:

Businesses must prioritize the integration of AI into their operations to enhance resource efficiency, minimize waste, and create circular supply chains. This requires investments in technology, training, and collaboration with technology providers.

2. Developing Circular Business Models:

Organizations should adopt circular business models, such as product-as-a-service, sharing platforms, and reverse logistics systems. AI-powered tools can optimize these models, enabling businesses to achieve economic growth while contributing to sustainability.

3. Collaboration Across Sectors:

Partnering with other industries, academic institutions, and governments can foster innovation and share best practices for scaling AI-driven CE solutions. Collaborative initiatives can address shared challenges and accelerate progress.

4. Transparency and Accountability:

Businesses must ensure transparency in their operations by leveraging AI to track resource flows and measure environmental impacts. Adopting ethical AI practices and reporting progress toward sustainability goals builds trust among stakeholders.

Society: Supporting Sustainable Practices

Individuals and communities play a critical role in supporting the transition to a CE enabled by AI. Societal engagement and behavioral changes are essential for the success of these initiatives.

1. Adopting Sustainable Lifestyles:

Consumers should make conscious choices to support sustainable products, participate in recycling programs, and reduce waste. AI-driven applications can empower individuals with insights and recommendations for adopting environmentally friendly behaviors.

2. Advocating for Change:

Communities can advocate for policies and business practices that align with CE principles. Public demand for sustainable products and services creates market incentives for businesses to innovate.

3. Participating in Education and Awareness:

Society must prioritize education and awareness to understand the benefits of AI and CE. Engaging in discussions and workshops on sustainability can help communities contribute actively to the transition.

Collaboration for a Sustainable Future

The success of AI-driven CE systems depends on the coordinated efforts of all stakeholders. Governments must create enabling environments, businesses must drive innovation, and society must support and adopt sustainable practices. By working together, we can unlock the transformative potential of AI to build a sustainable and equitable global economy that preserves resources for future generations. This collective action is essential to address the pressing environmental challenges of our time and create a resilient future for all.